Divided Nations

'At a time when, as Ian Goldin argues, global politics is gridlocked, we need greater international co-operation than ever before - and the institutions to sustain it - in order to cope with the sort of problems from economic imbalances to the environment which individual nation states cannot overcome on their own. Ian Goldin shows why this is imperative and how it could be done. We must hope that his optimism that the international community will wake up and act before it is too late is not misplaced. After all, there is, as was once famously said, no alternative.'
Lord Chris Patten, Chancellor, University of Oxford

'Ian Goldin stylishly describes the Gordian knot of international governance and makes some sensible suggestions on how it might be cut.'
Lord Mark Malloch-Brown, former UN Deputy Secretary-General

Previous Publications by Ian Goldin

DIVIDED
NATIONS

Why Global Governance
is Failing, and What We Can Do
About It

IAN GOLDIN

OXFORD
UNIVERSITY PRESS

OXFORD
UNIVERSITY PRESS

Great Clarendon Street, Oxford, OX2 6DP,
United Kingdom

Oxford University Press is a department of the University of Oxford.
It furthers the University's objective of excellence in research, scholarship,
and education by publishing worldwide. Oxford is a registered trade mark of
Oxford University Press in the UK and in certain other countries

First Edition published in 2013

Impression: 1

British Library Cataloguing in Publication Data

Data available

Library of Congress Cataloging in Publication Data

Data available

ISBN 978-0-19-969390-0

Printed in Great Britain by
Clays Ltd, St Ives plc

To

Tess, Olivia, Alex,
and my sister Jaqui

CONTENTS

CONTENTS

LIST OF FIGURES

LIST OF ACRONYMS AND ABBREVIATIONS

APEC	Asia-Pacific Economic Cooperation
ASEAN	Association of Southeast Asian Nations
BCE	before common era
CDOs	collateralized debt obligations
EBRD	European Bank for Reconstruction and Development
EU	European Union
FAO	Food and Agriculture Organization (of the United Nations)
FDI	foreign direct investment
G8	Group of Eight (US, France, UK, Germany, Japan, Italy, Canada, Russia)
G20	Group of Twenty
GATT	General Agreement on Tariffs and Trade
GCIM	Global Commission on International Migration
GDP	gross domestic product
HIV/AIDS	Human Immunodeficiency Virus/ Acquired Immune Deficiency Syndrome
ICAO	International Civil Aviation Authority
IMF	International Monetary Fund
IOM	International Organization for Migration
IP	intellectual property
IPCC	Intergovernmenatl Panel on Climate Change
MDGs	Millennium Development Goals

MERCOSUR	Southern Common Market
MIT	Massachusetts Institute of Technology
NAFTA	North American Free Trade Agreement
NGO	non-governmental organization
OECD	Organisation for Economic Co-operation and Development
TED	Technology, Entertainment and Design
TNC	transnational corporation
UN	United Nations
UNCTAD	United Nations Conference on Trade and Development
UNDP	United Nations Development Programme
UNHCR	United Nations High Commissioner for Refugees
UNEP	United Nations Environment Programme
USSR	Union of Soviet Socialist Republics
WHO	World Health Organization
WTO	World Trade Organization

PREFACE AND ACKNOWLEDGEMENTS

This book draws on my personal experience over the past decades in addressing key challenges of global governance. I have been most fortunate to work with inspirational leaders, notably President Mandela, as well as many brilliant and committed individuals who have devoted years of their lives seeking to address global problems, ranging from poverty and pandemics to climate change and nuclear disarmament.

This book draws on observations I have accumulated in a variety of contexts. As Vice President and Director of Policy for the World Bank Group I participated in the Monterrey and numerous other global meetings devoted to reducing poverty and addressing global problems. As Special Representative to the United Nations, I served on the Chief Executive Board, chaired by the Secretary General, and on the UN Reform Task Force, chaired by the Prime Minister of Norway. In South Africa, as Advisor to President Mandela and Chief Executive of the Development Bank of Southern Africa, I negotiated on a number of global issues on behalf of the government. Previously, I had worked at the Organisation for Economic Co-operation and Development where I had been intimately involved in the Uruguay Round of trade negotiations. At the European Bank for Reconstruction and Development I had been involved in discussions on the accession of Eastern European countries to the European Union and on their participation in a wide range of environmental and other treaties.

Since 2006, I have served as Director of the Oxford Martin School at the University of Oxford. The School provides an extraordinarily stimulating and rich source of analysis regarding global challenges. Over 400 scholars from twenty-five disciplines work in forty overlapping teams that seek to identify and provide fresh and forward-looking perspectives on the greatest challenges facing humanity. The issues we are addressing touch on questions of health and medicine, science, governance and technology, environment and energy, demography, migration, and ageing, as well as questions of natural resources and food. Our research includes key questions regarding the future of globalization, and not least poverty, employment, and inequality. A programme on complexity, risk, and resilience has recently been initiated.

As we work on the many global challenges we are struck by the need for global solutions. If there is one thing that keeps us awake at night, it is the absence of global leadership and even awareness of the scale of the global challenges. James Martin, whose vision and generosity created the Oxford Martin School, notes that humanity is at a crossroads. This could be our best century ever, as we find the means and collective will to overcome poverty, disease, and many of the other tribulations that remain endemic despite human progress. Or it could be our worst century, as systemic risks and the unintended consequences of technological progress and globalization overwhelm the gains and lead to devastating destruction. The outcome will depend on our collective ability to understand and take action to address key challenges. It depends on global management. The widening gap between our knowledge of the issues and the failure of global leaders to address global concerns is our biggest challenge and the reason I have written this book.

I could not wish for more informed or concerned colleagues. This book draws on their tremendous expertise and patience in helping me to navigate the complexities of their topics.

Oxford University offers a wonderful source of research support. David Goll and Alex Barker worked for a number of months on this book, trawling the sources and contributing inputs in areas that have enriched the text. Subsequently, Abilene Pitt has filled in a number of holes and assisted in collating the graphics and references for the text and Karim Pal has diligently helped to ensure the consistency of the final text. My greatest debt is to Natalie Day, whose day job is Head of Policy for the Oxford Martin School. Starting with constructive criticism of early drafts, Natalie has contributed to both the style and substance, while providing a most helpful sounding board, squashing some of my most speculative ideas, and adding more sensible ones of her own.

Other colleagues in the Oxford Martin School have provided a highly supportive working environment. In particular, Laura Lauer, the School's administrator, has provided a stable foundation for my activities. Lindsay Walker, Verity Ross-Smith, and Claire-Louise Jordan have juggled my work schedule and through the effectiveness of their support have kept me in good humour.

Latha Menon at Oxford University Press has broken the mould to initiate a new series of books with the Oxford Martin School, of which this is the first. Her incisive comments and editing have provided a consummate professional's improvement to the text. Emma Marchant and Jennifer Lunsford at OUP have provided highly effective guidance and support throughout the publication process, and Dan Harding's proof-reading and Elizabath Stone's copy-editing have served to polish the manuscript. Credit is due too to Alison Stibbe, the Head of Communications, for curating this new book series for the Oxford Martin School. Our hope is that this will be the first in a series of volumes that extend the debates and research taking place within the Oxford Martin School to a wider audience. Each volume is the responsibility of individual Oxford professors rather than representing a collective view, and the perspectives, errors, and omissions in this volume are solely attributable to me.

This book has been written in the evenings and weekends and during my holidays. My family has inevitably suffered most from this commitment and it is to Tess, Olivia, and Alex that I give my heartfelt thanks for allowing me once again to plunge into another book. My hope is that the ideas I have outlined here will raise awareness regarding the need for radical improvements in global governance, and that in so doing I contribute to a better life for the current and for future generations.

Ian Goldin

Oxford, July 2012.

CHAPTER ONE

New Global Governance Challenges

Unfit for Purpose

I wrote this book because I believe that increasingly globalization presents a paradox: it has been the most progressive force in history, but the most severe crises of the 21st century will arise due to the very success of globalization. Unless we are able to manage these threats, there is a real danger that globalization will have given birth to its own downfall. A succession of crises that result from increased integration will lead to a backlash. Citizens will see increased integration as too risky. They will become increasingly xenophobic, protectionist, and nationalist. Our integrated financial and trade systems, and other networks such as energy systems and the internet, could become fragmented into silos.

This would be disastrous, as it would lead to a downward spiral and the arresting of the opportunities offered by globalization. Poor people, as always, would be the first to suffer the consequences, with their livelihoods and prospects undermined by slower global growth and the perversely regressive impacts of insularity.

The stakes could not be higher. Unless we are able to more effectively manage the risks associated with globalization, they will overwhelm us. This is the core challenge of our times.

The 20th century was characterized by at least four terrible global tragedies. Two brutal world wars, a global pandemic, and a worldwide depression affected almost everyone on the planet. In response to these and other crises the United Nations (UN), Bretton Woods (the World Bank and International Monetary Fund), and other international institutions were created which aimed to ensure that humanity never faced crises on the same scale again.

These institutions have enjoyed some success. After all, we are yet to witness another global conflict despite decades of Cold War tension between competing superpowers. Until 2008, modern-day recessions had not come close to the deep worldwide contraction created by the Great Depression, for which the International Monetary Fund (IMF) and World Bank can claim some credit. The World Health Organization (WHO) and other agencies may also take pride in having overcome polio, smallpox, and a number of other devastating communicable diseases and preventing a significant global pandemic despite increasing connectivity and population density.

The future, however, will be unlike the past. We face a new set of challenges. The biggest of these is that our capacity to manage global issues has not kept pace with the growth in their complexity and danger. Global institutions which may have had some success in the 20th century are now unfit for purpose. The repurposing of global governance to meet the new challenges is a vital and massive undertaking. Responsibility for this revolution lies not just with the global governance organizations themselves, or indeed with national governments.

Nations are divided and cannot agree a common approach, and within the leading nations there is no consensus or leadership on critical global issues. The continued failure to resolve the financial crisis which started in 2007, the impasse in climate and environment negotiations at the Rio+20 conference in 2012 and the Durban conference in 2011, as well as the stymied 'development round' of trade negotiations initiated in Doha in 2001 should be a wake-up call to us all.

Global governance is at a crossroads and appears incapable of overcoming the current gridlock in the most significant global negotiations. The number of countries involved in negotiations (close to 200 now) and the complexity of the issues and their interconnectedness have grown rapidly, as has the effect of instant media and other pressures on politicians. These and other factors have paralysed progress, so the prospect of resolving critical global challenges appears ever more distant. We have reached a fork in the road. New solutions must be found.

Resolving questions of global governance urgently requires an invigorated national and global debate. This necessitates the involvement of ordinary citizens everywhere. For without the engagement and support of us all, reform efforts are bound to fail.

Structural changes in the world have led to fundamental shifts in the nature of the challenges and their potential for resolution. In this book I select five key challenges for this century—climate change, cybersecurity, pandemics, migration, and finance—to illustrate the need for fundamental reform of global governance. I am not suggesting that these issues are completely new. It is the radical change in the nature of these challenges and the complexity and potential severity of their impact that defines them as 21st-century challenges.

The UN, WHO, IMF, World Trade Organization (WTO), and other institutions charged with global governance have undertaken reform at a painfully slow pace. The growing disconnect between the need for urgent collective decision making to meet 21st-century challenges and the evolutionary progress in institutional capability has led to a yawning governance gap.

This book seeks to identify the growing gap between yesterday's structures and today's problems, and provides perspectives on possible future solutions. By global governance, I mean the institutions and processes which seek to manage global problems. Global implies they transcend national and regional borders and involve many countries. This definition captures traditional global governance structures, including the institutions already referred to, such as the UN, WTO, IMF, and WHO. It also refers to the different players that participate and influence global governance and the management of global issues including regional alliances, the nation state, and private–public partnerships at the global level as well as civil-society engagement in global affairs.

My aim is not to be comprehensive or add to the exhaustive analysis of the existing global governance arrangements. Libraries are filled with books on the many hundreds of international organizations, treaties, and agreements that seek to manage global affairs. Rather, this book offers fresh perspectives on these organizations in light of today's challenges, and makes proposals that aim to contribute to the resolution of these challenges, both through the reform of these traditional structures and by alternative means.

A Hyper-connected Age

During the latter half of the 20th century, cross-border connections between individuals multiplied. As interconnectivity mushroomed, so did the mandates facing the international institutions. Technological change coupled with the toxic politics of the Cold War threatened the lives of individuals across the world. Nuclear proliferation and the rising pressures of the Cold War brought with them the real and ever-present possibility of mutually assured destruction.

In the two decades since the fall of the Berlin Wall, fundamental political, economic, and technological changes have led to a step-change in global connectivity. Interdependence and innovation have brought unprecedented benefits, and led to the most rapid global rise in incomes and health in history. However, the same processes of integration and innovation have also greatly increased the potential for systemic risk and global crises. Globalization is leaping ahead of the lethargic institutions of global governance.

In politics, the collapse of the Soviet Union, the opening up of China, the integration of the EU, and the ending of totalitarian regimes in over seventy countries, have facilitated both physical and virtual connectivity. They have also meant that citizens are now aware and potentially engaged with matters that are beyond the borders of their nation states. Technological change, and notably the development of fibre optics, the internet, containerization, and cheaper flights, have brought people physically and virtually closer together. Economic reform has been associated with the reduction in barriers to trade and financial flows. A virtuous circle of increasing levels of education and infrastructure in emerging economies has been associated with rapidly rising living standards and incomes through much of the developing world.

Despite all the progress made in development, intractable poverty must remain a central concern of a civilized world. Over a billion people still live on a dollar a day or less, and over two billion on less than two dollars. For many of these people, the problem is too little, not too much, connectivity. They are isolated by geography, lack of infrastructure, or illiteracy. Too many governments also fail to transmit the benefits and possibilities of globalization to their citizens, as is the case, for example in resource-rich countries where a small elite group capture the benefits of oil, minerals, or other exports.

Fortunately, even for people living in totalitarian and isolated places, the walls which divide are crumbling. We now live in an age of hyper-connectivity: states, institutions, and individuals are connected to each other as never before. The trends which first emerged in the latter half of the 20th century—increased linkages through transport and trade—have accelerated. Integration has brought immense benefits to many, but has created a new breed of risk at the same time as it creates new opportunities. Actions taken by any one country, and indeed by a single individual or firm, now have the potential to cascade globally. The level of interdependence has multiplied. So too have the externalities, or spill-over effects, arising from turbo-charged globalization.

While the physical and virtual connections have multiplied, the necessary political and institutional reforms required to manage increased integration have lagged. Urgent attention needs to be given to both the upside and downside of increasing connectedness.

At the national level, the biggest challenge for politicians and policy makers is the need to balance the enormous benefits that global openness and connectivity bring, with national politics and priorities. This also is a major concern for citizens, who are torn between the benefits of imported goods and services, and their worries about local jobs, illicit flows, and other implications of more open borders. These concerns are universal and affect all societies.

Globalization is a generator of tremendously positive but also highly negative forces. For example, the increasing openness and integration of the Chinese economy has been associated with over 600 million Chinese people escaping dire poverty and the Chinese economy tripling in size over the past twenty-five years. China will, over the coming decades, overtake the US to become the largest economy. While the beneficial effects of growth include poverty reduction and the stabilizing role of China in the world economy, the downside risks have also multiplied. Already, the associated growth in carbon consumption has propelled China to become the world's largest emitter of greenhouse gases. Global governance will have to confront the escalating dangers of climate change, collapsing biodiversity, and other failures of the global commons that result from the combination of long-term increases in consumption in the richer countries and the now rapid acceleration of consumption in emerging markets.

The escalation of the global challenges is in large part the underbelly of accelerated globalization. Unless these can be managed more effectively and proactively, nations and citizens around the world will turn their backs on globalization. The result will be an increasing desire to slam shut the doors of globalization.

Rearranging the Deckchairs

The treaties and other agreements that global governance structures have spawned are at best able to deal with a number of key challenges from the past. More often than not they are ignored or violated. Perpetual talk of reform and a myriad of costly international meetings have led to a well-worn cynicism about international reform efforts. These have been associated with a stuttering evolution of the international system and even the occasional appearance of new institutions.

Few, if any, international organizations have been closed down during the past sixty years, but many have withered and faded into irrelevance, kept on drip feed by their host countries or a handful of governments with vested interests. Thousands of international meetings, civil society organizations, and scholars have focused on the necessary reform of the existing institutions. I served on the UN reform initiative that the then Secretary-General Kofi Annan initiated. Despite the active participation of a number of Prime Ministers and numerous experts, and some marginal reform, the bulk of the reform proposals, like those of prior reform efforts, are gathering dust on a UN shelf.

Too often reforms in global governance are equivalent to rearranging the deckchairs on the *Titanic*. Much bigger threats loom than those that are the focus of these earnest efforts. The world has changed in fundamental ways since the institutions were formed and so it should come as no surprise that they are overwhelmed by new challenges. Concerted reform may in some areas close the governance gap, but for the most part the participants in these reform efforts include representatives of the governments who have resisted reform and so significant reform is stymied. As a result, across the existing system the governance gap is already too wide, and widening.

Our focus is on the governance gap that pertains to new challenges. However, I am not complacent about the well-established systems. For example, even a cursory look at the system with respect to nuclear arms shows how we cannot take much comfort from its relative success in preventing a nuclear war. The establishment of a global institutional arrangement that would facilitate the peaceful and safe use of nuclear energy and all nuclear weapons is urgently required. There are currently no binding international agreements on how to protect nuclear material stored within home countries; a UN agreement seeking to address this critical area has still not been ratified after seven years.[1] Given the significant international security risks associated with nuclear energy and weapons, it is alarming that there has not been more global progress on this critical issue.

Learn from Post and Planes

Not all global institutions have failed to keep pace with the times, and there are notable exceptions. The International Civil Aviation

Authority (ICAO) and the Universal Postal Union have adapted to revolutions in politics and shifts in geographical borders and technologies with remarkable agility. And there are many other examples of standards-based international systems which are mutually beneficial and which operate relatively effectively. No country would benefit from applying different rules. We must ask what we can learn from these examples of what psychologists may see as organizations which establish superordinate goals, where individuals and nations voluntarily subordinate themselves to shared collective outcomes.

This book provides a number of illustrations of areas where the governance deficit is particularly wide. It is necessarily far from comprehensive. I do not deal with many of the vital but well-covered global issues that others have addressed. These include poverty, human rights, nuclear proliferation, water and food security, and a host of other critical issues. My aim is to look forward and highlight as indicative a number of the new challenges to global governance. Any text is necessarily selective. An overview on a vast topic may be expected to be even more so.

Book Outline

In the remainder of Chapter 1, I outline a number of the new dangers posed by hyper-connectivity. I cite the examples of our growing vulnerability to financial crisis, pandemic, and cyberattack, as well as the dangers resulting from the failure to collectively manage migration and climate change.

Chapter 2 examines whether our existing multilateral institutions can deal with these issues, or whether we will have to look for other solutions. I also examine the role of regional and interest-based grouping in these debates.

Chapter 3 considers some promising proposals for change in global governance, looking firstly at the crucial reforms needed for existing institutions to become more relevant, and then further afield for more creative approaches. Chapter 4 considers the impact of globalization on the individual. Individuals enjoy more power than ever before due to the potential for their voice, to ripple globally. I consider whether this is good or bad and how the rising power of individuals may help solve global problems. Chapter 5 draws together the insights from the previous chapters to offer a roadmap for the future of global governance.

The New Challenges Facing Global Governance

Let us now consider five new 21st-century global challenges in turn, starting with the financial crisis.

The far-reaching consequences of the initial shock emanating from the subprime mortgage crisis are indicative of a wider trend. Increasingly, local hazards are becoming global problems, whether it is the collapse of a housing market, the outbreak of a pathogen, or a computer virus that can spread across the world in a matter of hours. These systemic threats share a number of common features, and they pose a new form of global challenge. As we become more interconnected the previously domestic concerns of sovereign states have spilled over to affect the well-being of individuals and countries that previously were insulated from the risks. Increased interconnectivity and complexity has engendered a new cascading form of risk.

The positive externalities include a leap in the potential for global innovation and poverty reduction. The negative externalities include a severe increase in the risk of catastrophic systemic risks. In the next chapters, I will consider these challenges in the context of existing governance frameworks, their relationship to individual power, and possibilities for reform. But first let us set these discussions in context.

Finance

The financial crisis that started in 2008 was the first of the systemic crises of the 21st century. It will not be the last. Indeed, it is unfortunately a harbinger of new forms of systemic risk.[2] We see in finance, as we do in other areas, the potent blend of sharply rising connectivity, derived from accelerated globalization and technological change (in the case of financial instruments derived from the exponential growth of computing power), in combination with institutional capture and the political failure to comprehend, let alone prevent, the growing threat.

The financial crisis took many people by surprise. It came at the end of a decade of prosperity for many Western economies. Output growth was steady. Inflation was low. The 'golden decade' that came to an abrupt end in 2008 reflected the success of globalization. During this period economic growth accelerated rapidly in many developing countries. More open, globally integrated economies were rewarded with higher growth. This appeared to confirm the wisdom of economists who argued for more open markets and freer trade.

Conditions were benign enough to earn the period a moniker that, with hindsight, has come to appear severely ironic: 'the great moderation'. Some economists went even further. Robert Lucas, a Nobel Prize winner, claimed in his 2003 presidential address to the American Economic Association that the 'central problem of depression-prevention has been solved ... and has in fact been solved for many decades'.[3]

The financial services industry was booming. They had discovered a new business model that allowed them to realize profits far beyond those available within other sectors. The cornerstone of this model was a traditional financial product: the mortgage. Due to inflows of surplus savings, mainly from China, mortgages could be extended to a wider range of customers than ever before. The extension of home-ownership suited the government of the US: loose credit raised the living standards of the poor and softened the impact of increased wage inequality. They accelerated financial deregulation and, through the government guaranteed Fannie Mae and Freddie Mac agencies, propped up the growing market for mortgages.

Lenders did not, for the most part, hold on to mortgages. Instead, they packaged them into 'collateralized debt obligations' (CDOs)—securities that provided a flow of cash to investors through the returns on a large number of assets, both high- and low-risk. CDOs with a variety of different assets weren't as risky as the mortgages they contained and offered flexibility. The level of risk borne by investors could be tailored to their demand.

Investment in CDOs grew exponentially. In 2004, global CDO issues were valued at $157.4 billion. By 2006, this number had grown to $520.6 billion.[4] A large portion of these CDOs were structured around subprime lending. As the international appetite for CDOs grew, it became increasingly easy to sell on high-risk mortgages. As a result, lenders started to target individuals with little or no means to make repayments.

The subprime crisis was the tipping point. As interest rates were increased by the Federal Reserve, individuals on variable-rate mortgages found themselves unable to keep up their payments. Defaults became widespread and house prices plummeted. As a result, the CDOs became increasingly worthless—a collapse in the mortgage market meant that there was no money to meet the obligations. The ensuing crisis has resulted in trillions of dollars worth of damage. Competitive pressures for short-term gains had rendered the system taut. Eventually a small change in conditions tipped the whole system into freefall.

The domino effect

Why did the collapse of a relatively small asset market have such wide-ranging and dramatic consequences? The driving force behind the spread of the contagion was the increased connectivity between financial institutions. Banks have built a complex web of obligations, assets, and interdependencies. As a result, the collapse of a few banks central to the global financial system resulted in a domino effect. At first, banks failed because their business model relied on the ability to sell mortgages on. But very quickly, banks were failing because other banks were failing.

Specifically, the collapse of the subprime market led to a dangerous freeze in interbank lending. Each bank was unsure about the amount of CDOs held by other banks, and therefore the exposure of each bank to subprime losses. The increased risk associated with lending to other banks caused the interest rates on interbank lending to skyrocket. Many banks were left with mortgages they were unable to sell, short-term debts they were unable to pay, and no line of credit to see them through the crisis.

The problems were not limited to the US. Banks across the world were revealed to be heavily involved in CDOs. In fact, the first casualty of the subprime crisis was a British bank. As the demand for securities caved in, Northern Rock was forced to appeal for a loan from the Bank of England. This resulted in a classic bank run and eventually led to Northern Rock being nationalized.

Over the next few months, banks were acquired or bankrupted in the US, Iceland, the Netherlands, Belgium, Ireland, and Spain. As highlighted in Figure 1, the interdependencies of the global finance network left countries across the world vulnerable to large financial shocks.

Even the banks with relatively healthy balance sheets found themselves unable to borrow at reasonable rates, and therefore were unwilling to extend credit to their customers. Investment plummeted. Falling house-prices meant that consumers felt poorer, and uncertainty about the future availability of credit meant that they were unwilling to spend. Consumption collapsed, and economies spiralled into decline.

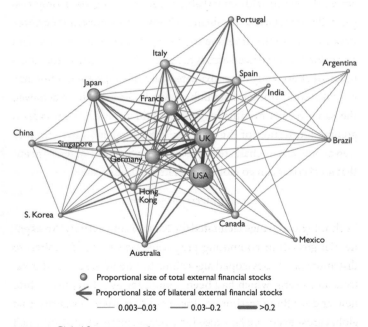

FIGURE 1 Global finance network

Andrew G. Haldane, 2009. Executive Director, Bank of England. 'Rethinking the Financial Network'.

This created a vicious circle: bank failure led to economic decline, economic decline led to a sharp fall in the value of assets, the fall in the value of assets led to further bank failure. The country hit hardest by the financial crisis was the US, whose consumption had previously fuelled the export-driven economies of Europe and Asia. World output per capita fell in 2009 for the first time since 1982.[5]

The shape of the financial crisis is recognizable—an asset bubble in the housing market propelled by excess credit. There are parallels with the Asian financial crisis of 1997, but the depth and the breadth far exceeded what we had seen previously. The contagion swept across the world with remarkable speed, reaching areas only tangentially connected to the financial hubs of New York and London. Few countries were immune to the rapid decline in employment and growth experienced across the globe. The collapse in the housing market was only the proximate cause; if subprime lending had not taken off, another asset bubble would probably have achieved the same results eventually. The 2008 financial crisis provides a graphic illustration of the potential for contagion—the complex web of obligations characteristic of modern financial systems means that local crises can go global in a matter of hours.

Local showers, global storms

Technological change facilitated the leaps in connectivity. An exponential growth in computing processing power was exploited to distribute newly developed algorithms to extend the use of derivatives and swaps, which had been around for over forty years, into new and far-flung territories. The regulators were not aware that global gross exposure far exceeded global income. Or that over half of a key element of derivative traffic was routed through one node, Lehman Brothers.

The information needed to understand this was available. The failure to manage the system was not due to an absence of data. Finance prided itself as the best equipped and best governed of the international and national systems of governance. The treasuries, securities exchange, Federal Reserve, Bank for International Settlements and IMF, and the central banks and finance ministries around the world are the elite of national and global governance. They have the best people, with the best resources, the most data and the most effective networks, both at the national level and in terms of the global institutions. Relative to all other national and global surveillance systems, finance was, and remains, the best endowed. Yet this system of governance was found to be totally unfit for 21st-century purpose. They simply did not see the crisis coming. And when it came, they were unable to arrest or, to this day, address its underlying causes.

Looking ahead, serious challenges to financial stability are likely to emerge from novel financial instruments that bypass existing legislation. There are parallels here between the competitive pressures of a market economy and the evolutionary pressures of natural selection. Profitable financial innovations spread and multiply in the same way that successful mutations dissipate. Financiers face similar incentives to find and exploit weaknesses in regulation. High-performing graduates are recruited as financial engineers with a mandate to devise products that, while legal, exploit the possibilities of new technological opportunities and loopholes in legislation. Since young graduates are in an innovation race with ageing regulators operating within the confines of their national borders, the potential for regulatory arbitrage is growing. As these instruments become more complex, the dangers they pose are harder to counteract.

In the recent crisis, CDOs played the role of the pathogen. Little understood, they allowed banks to greatly increase exposure to risk under the collective nose of the world's most revered financial economists and central bankers. We must expect further innovations in the future. As long as there is a significant financial return to tools that allow banks to circumvent regulation, the best and the brightest will be tasked with their invention.

Tipping points and positive feedback loops are clearly manifested in financial markets. A booming asset market will tend to grow for as long as investors expect it to grow. High levels of investment drive up prices, and increasing prices attract more investors to the market. Each effect drives the other. This loop continues until some unexpected event changes expectations. At that point, the concerns of investors become self-fulfilling—as they scramble to get out of the market prices start to collapse, and as prices collapse it becomes even more important to get out.

As a result, both systems can be extremely unpredictable. The challenge goes beyond that of better coordination, since a failure to understand how complex systems have evolved lies at the root of the problem. We need to increase our understanding of how each system works, and be alert to future rapid changes in the technologies and networks that underpin their rapid evolution. This is often easier said than done. The financial crisis has demonstrated that even the best equipped of the systems—the elite of global institutions, people, and data—could not keep pace with rapid changes associated with globalization and technical change.

Silver linings

The solution is not to cut back on globalization and connectivity. While it may be easy to dismiss the gains from financial connectivity in the face of the recent crisis, there are good reasons to expect that they could also be substantial. Access to credit and investment can be an engine of growth, provided it is properly managed, and interconnected financial institutions could be able to help millions of individuals lift themselves out of poverty.

The lack of access to credit in developing countries is often a major barrier to growth and driver of poverty. This insight has provided the foundation for the growing 'microcredit' movement. Institutions such as the Grameen Bank have been able to provide astonishing gains for the poorest individuals through the increased availability of small loans.

Other capital flows should also be able to reduce poverty in low-income countries. Large-scale investment by multinational corporations can be destructive of local interests if it compromises the natural environment, or increases the dominance of a foreign culture over that of the host country. But it can also bring direct and indirect benefits, including promoting competition, transferring technology, and improving the wages and training of local employees.

In the book I have co-authored with Kenneth Reinert, *Globalization for Development: Meeting New Challenges*, we demonstrate just how important the creation of local capital markets is for development. We encourage countries to develop a balance between their reliance on commercial banks, bond markets, equity investments, and foreign investment, highlighting the importance of heterodox policies on the development of domestic capital markets and their integration into the international system.[6]

To ensure that the positive impact overwhelms the threats, this book argues that a new form of global governance, fit for 21st-century purpose, is required. In the case of finance, governance reform remained national and lagged behind technological and other global advances which facilitated a financial boom. The result was a catastrophic financial bust.

Pandemics

Even more worrying than the consequences of systemic risk in finance is the potential impact of pandemics. Influenza pandemics, like financial crises, are not in themselves new—there have been nine major pandemics caused by influenza in the past three centuries.

The unpredictable threat posed by pandemics is associated with the ability of large portions of the population to develop resistance to the more prevalent strains of influenza, so each pandemic is the result of the evolution of a new strain and each strain varies in its lethality and contagiousness.

The real challenge posed by new strains of influenza is a result of their novelty. Viruses constantly evolve through a process of mutation. Often the mutations will be disadvantageous to the virus, but occasionally mutations will arise that allow the virus to reproduce more effectively. A similar process occurs in bacterial diseases.

New strains are biologically different from those observed previously, so existing immunities and vaccines tend to be ineffective. Vaccinations have to be designed and produced before they can be deployed. By this point, the pandemic is often already widespread.

The earliest confirmed case of the 2009 outbreak of influenza A (H1N1), commonly known as 'swine flu', was recorded on 17 March 2009 in Mexico.[7] Swine flu is particularly contagious, although its virulence is low. The pathogen spreads rapidly. By 28 March there was a recorded case in the US.[8] A month later, cases had been confirmed in Canada, Spain, the United Kingdom, Israel, and New Zealand.[9] By the time the WHO declared the outbreak a pandemic on 11 June, seventy-four countries had reported over 25,000 cases of swine flu.[10]

The situation got worse before it got better. The infection continued to spread, despite growing concern from officials and the public. Mass vaccinations didn't begin until September—first in the US, followed shortly by Australia. At this point, almost 4,000 people had been killed.[11]

The pandemic eventually began to subside. There was growing immunity among the public—partly because of the vaccinations, partly because of the natural immunity among those who had already been infected. The pandemic is estimated by the WHO to have caused at least 18,000 deaths, but a recent study from the Centre for Disease Control in Atlanta has indicated the actual figure may have been fifteen times larger at around 300,000 deaths.[12]

Better swine than Spanish

Compared with previous influenza pandemics, this was an exceptionally fortunate result. The Spanish flu of 1918 (another H1N1 strain of influenza) is estimated to have infected around a third of the world's population and killed at least fifty million people.[13] How did we subsequently avoid such catastrophic losses?

Improvements in health care certainly contributed to a lower infection rate. However, the greatest contribution was a matter of luck rather than exemplary practice. The 2009 strain of influenza was relatively benign. It tended to kill only the very young and old, as with most types of influenza. The case fatality rate is estimated to be below 0.03 per cent.

Spanish flu, on the other hand, was remarkable in its lethality. Case fatalities exceeded 2.5 per cent. Some countries were decimated— the mortality rate in Western Samoa was 22 per cent.[14] Part of the increased mortality was the result of poor access to health care. However, there can be little doubt that the earlier pathogen was more dangerous. It had an unusual tendency to strike down individuals in the prime of their lives, especially pregnant mothers. Epidemiologists speculate that the virus tended to trigger an overreaction of the immune system that destroyed lung tissue.[15] Vigorous health could form as much of a disadvantage as profound weakness.

What would happen if a new strain of influenza, similar in virulence to the 1918 strain, was to emerge today? In 1918, the war created exceptional vulnerabilities that aided the spread of the pathogen, through troops moving around the world and living in unsanitary trench conditions. In peacetime, the pandemic would have had a much smaller impact. At that time far less than 1 per cent of the current number of people travelled internationally, and the war and resettlement of soldiers fostered the pandemic's spread. Nowadays it would go global virtually immediately. Indeed, the term 'viral' has been adopted to signify the rapid global reach of new blogs or images on social networks or through sharing on the Internet.

Your passport please

There are two major trends driving our increased exposure to lethal global pathogens. First, travel and transport networks allow pathogens to go global in a matter of days. Second, increased proximity through a combination of urbanization and population growth, as well as severely crowded living conditions in a growing number of cities, has the capacity to lead to the same patterns of transmission and mutation witnessed in the trenches.

International travel has exploded in recent years, with over 980 million tourist arrivals worldwide in 2011 alone.[16] Increases in income and improvements in infrastructure have greatly enhanced mobility. We have the technological capabilities to travel to distant countries faster and cheaper than before, and the combination of rising incomes, lower transport costs, the ending of political isolation, and improved facilities and security has meant that travel is increasing by more than 7 per cent per year, especially to previously remote locations, as depicted in Figure 2.

The growth in travel and increased competitive pressures have led to the creation of a number of transport 'hubs' through which a significant proportion of international and national travel is routed. For instance, more than 633 million passengers passed through the world's ten busiest airports in 2010 that include Atlanta, Beijing, Heathrow, Tokyo, and Paris.[17] These hubs have the potential to accelerate the spread of pandemics, as the infection is passed to individuals who return to their home country before developing symptoms.

This is exactly what happened during the H1N1 outbreak. As shown in Figure 3, the disease spread at an astonishing rate thanks to international flows of travellers and tourists. While we were thankfully spared catastrophic fatalities, it does not bode well for the future. If a more virulent strain were to emerge the outbreak would be worldwide and unpredictable.

The SARS and HIV/AIDS pandemics

This increased connectivity means that public health policy in one country can have implications for the health of individuals across the world. A key example is the severe acute respiratory syndrome, or SARS, pandemic.

SARS is a respiratory disease that originated in China around November 2002. As it spread, the Chinese authorities became increasingly aware that the pathogen represented a severe threat. They soon put measures in place to try and contain the outbreak but were also keen to suppress information related to the virus. There was a fear that releasing information may result in a panic, and that the consequences for the economy may be disastrous. For four months, information was kept under wraps. The result was that the

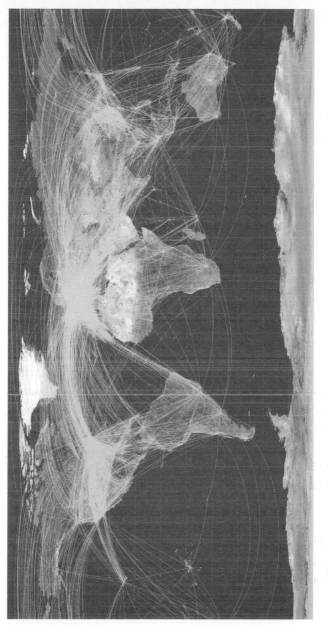

FIGURE 2 Global aviation network
VC Blog: Airline Routes

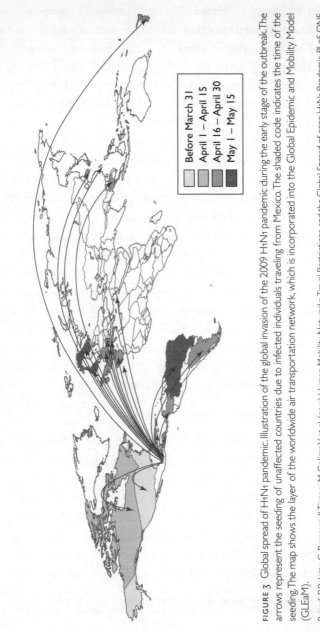

FIGURE 3 Global spread of H1N1 pandemic. Illustration of the global invasion of the 2009 H1N1 pandemic during the early stage of the outbreak. The arrows represent the seeding of unaffected countries due to infected individuals traveling from Mexico. The shaded code indicates the time of the seeding. The map shows the layer of the worldwide air transportation network, which is incorporated into the Global Epidemic and Mobility Model (GLEaM).

Bajardi P, Poletto C, Ramasco JJ, Tizzoni M, Colizza V, et al. (2011) Human Mobility Networks, Travel Restrictions, and the Global Spread of 2009 H1N1 Pandemic. PLoS ONE 6(1):e16591.

Legend:
- Before March 31
- April 1 – April 15
- April 16 – April 30
- May 1 – May 15

pathogen had time to spread. The suppression of information severely limited the ability of the WHO to take precautionary measures. Following a series of infections in the popular Metropole Hotel in Hong Kong, SARS was spread around the world (the hotel has subsequently rebranded itself as the Metropark Hotel). The pandemic caused hundreds of deaths—not only in China, but in Canada, Singapore, Taiwan, and Vietnam.

The HIV/AIDS pandemic was first identified in the US in 1969.[18] Its spread has reflected the nature of globalization and shows global inequities in wealth and well-being in sharp relief.[19] Given the nature of transmission, it differs from the management required in influenza outbreaks, where pathogens are largely airborne and spread rapidly. Instead, with approximately thirty-four million people living with HIV as of 2010,[20] management of this pandemic has become a political issue. With drugs and medical care, those with HIV now are able to live near to full life expectancy, but this is entirely dependent on access to such resources and the capacity of governments to provide it. HIV/AIDS is spread through human contact and highlights the significance of global travel and socioeconomic factors in the long-term management of pandemics once the initial containment and quarantine stages have passed.

Population, pathogen, and people power

Population growth, urbanization, and travel are increasing the risk of pandemics. The world population is predicted to grow by two to three billion in the coming forty years.[21] Almost all of this growth will be in developing countries, and almost all will be absorbed by cities. The world's rural population is likely to have already peaked. It will soon begin to decline. The world's urban population in 2050 will outnumber the rural eight to one.[22] This extraordinary growth of connectivity through urbanization greatly increases the risk of contagion, with local disasters escalating into global collapses.

Biological disasters also tend to be products of innovation. New pathogens are dangerous pathogens, and vice versa. Mutation creates a process of constant change, and the further removed a pathogen is from existing threats to our health, the more likely it is to cause widespread damage. Pathogens that successfully exploit weaknesses in our immunity will reproduce quickly and widely.

The acceleration of technical change beyond the evolutionary advance of supervisory authorities is a common feature of both the financial and biological systemic risks. It presents both a significant challenge, but also unprecedented opportunities for global governance.

In the case of pandemics, the exponential decline in the cost of

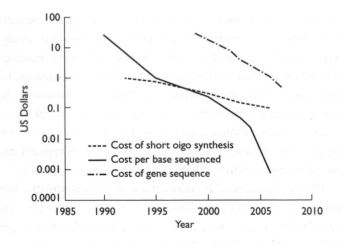

FIGURE 4 DNA sequencing cost
Rob Carlson, www. synthesis. cc.

DNA synthesizing is shown in Figure 4. This has created a new class of potential pandemic risks as small numbers of individuals, perhaps a single individual, are able to create a new bio-pathogen. The ability of individuals to manufacture smallpox, ebola, or even worse pandemic agents is a growing threat, as prices decline and availability of the necessary equipment and recipes spreads, including through the Internet. The policing of this lags well behind the rising threat, to the extent that it may already be too late to have prevented synthesis machines getting into the wrong hands. While governments have had the potential to create biological agents for many years, what is new is the ability of individuals to have this power and the potency of their own personal potential weapons of mass destruction.

Cybersecurity

A central theme of this book is the governance challenges associated with hyper-connectivity and accelerating technological change. Technological advances tend to be double-edged swords. In design, they are almost universally the product of well-meaning scientists and innovators, and in their application they have led to revolutions that have benefited all aspects of our lives. However, history is replete with examples of innovation that leads, either by design or by accident, to devastatingly negative consequences. Technologies are typically dual use, providing tools that can be used for immense good or harm.

The Internet is a revolutionary advance with transformative beneficial potential. Yet cybersecurity is a key challenge for local and global governance in the 21st century. Understanding how to prevent, or at least mitigate, the most systemically harmful consequences of the technological changes associated with the Internet and computing is still at a dangerous nascent stage.

Parallel to financial and physical connectivity, the Internet carries its own risks. As the number of institutions and individuals active on the Internet has increased, so have the gains to exploitation. This is partly because of an increased reliance on the efficiency gains offered by digitalization. Networked computers are used to provide public and private services that now permeate all aspects of our lives. Attacks have the potential to grind the entire system of commerce and social engagement as well as crucial public services, such as e-government, water, power, and communication, to a halt.

The dangers of overreliance on networked computers became evident following a series of attacks on Estonia in 2007. During a dispute with Russia over the removal of a Soviet statue the country suffered three successive waves of cyberaggression. Hackers used hundreds of thousands of captured 'zombie' computers to flood Estonia with Internet traffic. Dozens of websites were compromised, including the websites of the Estonian president, most of the government ministries, and two of the country's largest banks. It is unclear how deep the damage went, or to what extent networks were hijacked. There is no reliable estimate for the financial cost. However, Estonia is unusually dependent on e-commerce—for instance, 90 per cent of bank transactions are conducted online.[23] The damage is therefore likely to have been substantial.

Botnets are large networks of computers that, unbeknown to their users, can be remotely controlled to perform functions for the hackers who have commandeered them. Up to 80 per cent of the world's spam originates from bots. It is hard to estimate the number of computers that are under the control of hackers, but large botnets have often been composed of tens of millions of computers. The 'Waldec' botnet, shown in Figure 5, is an example of the reach of one such cyberinvasion.

Another risk is the targeting of government or industrial control systems. National e-government services as well as the national infrastructure, including power plants, electricity grids, and oil pipelines, use networked control systems to decrease operational costs. The concentration of information and power in these digital systems creates points of vulnerability, open to attack by malevolent forces.

The Stuxnet virus discovered in 2010 is widely thought to have caused damage to a uranium enrichment plant in Iran. Stuxnet is indicative of a new generation of viruses—professionally built and with the potential to damage systems that were previously considered impenetrable. The potential now exists for these to be contained in the software operating systems and also to be built into the hardware of machines, inserted at the time of manufacture of components or assembly.

Crime and non-punishment

Cyberaggression is one aspect of the cybersecurity problem. Stuxnet seems likely to have been created with the support of at least one government: the creators targeted a particular software and hardware set-up, suggesting detailed insider knowledge of a specific institution, and the complexity of the virus implies the work of a team of professionals over a number of months in order to damage the Iranian uranium-enrichment programme.

Another aspect of the cybersecurity problem is cybercrime. The division between cyberaggression and cybercrime is somewhat arbitrary, but I will use the latter to denote security threats motivated by financial gain and the former to denote acts with other motives. Cyberaggression can be launched from one state to

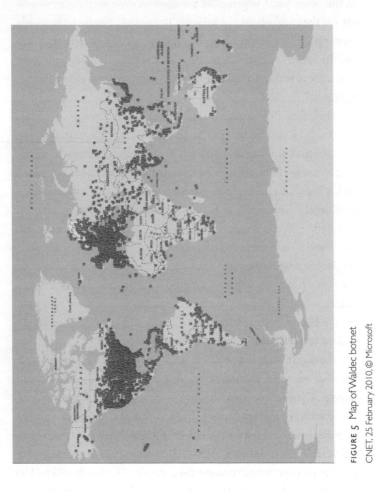

FIGURE 5 Map of Waldec botnet
CNET, 25 February 2010, © Microsoft

inconvenience or gain information from another, or by a group of individuals seeking to damage a particular institution. Cybercrime, on the other hand, is generally the work of groups of professionals out for their own financial benefit. The targets can be individuals, corporations, or institutions. The distinction is not meant to suggest the former is legal whereas the latter is not—both cyberaggression and cybercrime are illegal in most countries with cybersecurity legislation.

Cybercrime differs from that of conventional crime of the past in that it can be automated. For instance, emails are essentially costless, whether sending one or a million. Even if only one in 10,000 people are gullible enough to open an attachment that grants a hacker backdoor access to their computer, the scam will have been worthwhile. The result is that cybercrime affects every Internet user, rather than an unfortunate few. The number of people you know who have been personally affected by attempted or successful burglary is probably small. On the other hand, everyone who owns a personal computer will have suffered from thousands of attempted attacks, whether they are aware of this fact or not. Navigating cyberspace is becoming increasingly perilous—users must be constantly vigilant to avoid falling prey to criminal activity.

Cyberaggression is a problem because it could cause the breakdown of essential infrastructure systems or significant financial damage. Cybercrime is unlikely to cause this sort of systemic risk, as the attacks are uncoordinated. Instead, the real threat is that the inconvenience created for the individual will drive them from open and flexible machines such as the PC to more limited machines, and discourage experimentation on the Internet. The result will be less innovation and the gains to connectivity will not be maximized.

Users are already moving to increasingly 'tethered' machines, such as the iPad. The programmes that can run on the iPad are strictly controlled by the manufacturer, Apple. The result is that the individual is under little threat from viruses or spyware, but also that good code cannot be distributed easily. The uses of the iPad are directly controlled by one authority, ultimately motivated by the drive for profit. The uses of a PC are undefined—anyone can create code, adding functionality and improving performance.

Traditional tools to discourage aggressive and criminal behaviour are ineffective in cyberspace. The Internet allows attacks to be conducted under conditions of near perfect anonymity. It is very hard to trace the source of a particular security breach, since attacks are often conducted from compromised computers belonging to innocent bystanders. Even when an attack has been successfully traced, the evidence can be destroyed by a sophisticated cybercriminal. The damage can be compounded by the ability of a cyberattack to also promote misinformation that can potentially be used to cause panic, influence markets, and generally cause instability.

Deterrence is also rendered ineffective since crimes are generally multijurisdictional. An attacker residing in Russia can use compromised computers based in the US to launch an attack on Estonia. Even if authorities in Estonia managed to trace the attack back to Russia, how would they prosecute the criminal? Unless Russia wishes to cooperate, whether by extraditing the individual or prosecuting under their own laws, deterrence will be impossible. Unfortunately, cooperation is often denied—in fact, Russia did deny Estonia cooperation following the attacks of 2007 despite evidence that many of the attackers were Russian.

Tethered police

These two factors combine to render traditional security measures largely useless. An attacker residing in an uncooperative state knows that they are very unlikely to be brought to justice, and can therefore conduct criminal activity with very little fear of prosecution. The anonymity means that the military can use cyberweapons without fear of condemnation—there is almost no chance that any conclusive evidence could link the attacks back to them. And as the number of Internet users increases, the financial returns for cybercriminality look set to grow exponentially, drawing more individuals into the lucrative field. The problem of cybersecurity is therefore twofold. First, how do we minimize the risk of systemic breakdown due to cyberaggression? Second, how can we limit cybercrime while ensuring that the innovative capabilities of information and communication technology are preserved?

These complex cybersecurity issues transcend national boundaries and leave all countries vulnerable. While cybersecurity is emerging as a critical concern in the 21st century, there is currently no central governance agency focused on cybersecurity issues. We need a unified front in international policy and associated governance to monitor the growing evidence of cybervulnerability, deter cyber risks, and offer response support where attacks are successful. New models to understand and measure the relative effectiveness of protection strategies are needed, as well as global platforms through which to share best practice and data associated with cyberattacks.

Connectivity is not just important for the success of the Internet—connectivity is the Internet, and the Internet would be nothing without it. Yet, the same features that are essential for its existence also create its most serious threats. More than ever, criminals are able to act from relative safety, with little fear of retribution, in countries with little or no capability to find them and no incentive to cooperate with their victims.

In parallel to financial crises and pandemics, innovation is the key to the success of computer viruses and worms. Dangerous viruses utilize vulnerabilities in common programs and operating systems to gain access or cause damage to a machine. Once these viruses have been released, they can be analysed and the exploits, which are a sequence of commands which take advantage of the vulnerability, can be fixed. However, this process can take a while. By the time the update is released, effective viruses have often infected millions of machines, and since users do not update their programs regularly, it can continue spreading for months afterwards. Exceptionally dangerous viruses, like the so-called Code Red virus, the spread of which is depicted in Figure 6, can exploit a number of different vulnerabilities.

Reliance on the Internet also creates other points of vulnerability. Large underwater cables carry much of the digital information sent between continents. Damage to these cables has the ability to cause widespread 'Internet blackouts' across entire regions. In 2008 Internet services to the Middle East and South Asia were disrupted following the apparent breaking of the cables near the Suez Canal by ships' anchors. The following year, damage to a cable resulted in a complete loss of Internet service to several countries in Western Africa, and in subsequent years there have been a number of similar outages. We take for granted the ability to use networked computers. Finding global solutions to the growing vulnerability of these new arteries of global and national commerce and public services is essential if they are to continue to be a driving force of globalization and development.

The Changing Face of Migration

Migration is certainly not a new phenomenon, but the forces that have propelled migration in the past are continuing to intensify, and the sheer pressure of human movement requires that more attention be

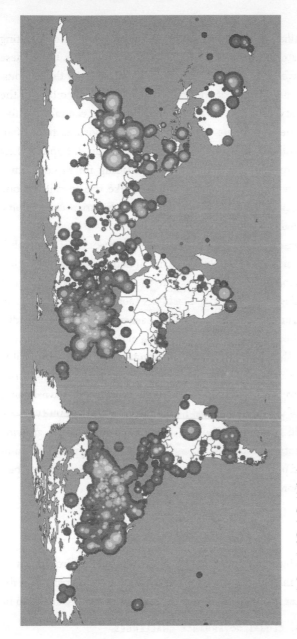

FIGURE 6 Spread of Code Red infections

paid to domestic policy and global migration governance.[24] People's ability to move from country to country, choosing where to build their lives and where to work, is a basic form of connectivity. As transport and communication prices fall, reducing the material and psychological cost of migration, we can expect demand for more open borders to expand. In 2010 there were over 220 million international migrants, more than double the figure recorded in 1980.[25] Like the connectivity of financial markets and of information, increased migration is essentially beneficial. The World Bank estimates that increasing migration by 3 per cent of the workforce in developed countries between 2005 and 2025 would result in global gains of US$356 billion, and completely opening borders over the next twenty-five years would yield the world economy an extra US$39 trillion and radically reduce poverty.[26]

Exceptional people

The key benefit of migration to the receiving country is that, by allowing people to move, it improves the welfare of the society as a whole. In *Exceptional People: How Migration Shaped Our World and Will Define our Future* my co-authors and I show that migration brings many benefits to the migrants and also to the host country, increasing the dynamism and growth potential of the receiving nation. Employing low-skilled migrants in low-skilled jobs can also allow natives to focus on the high-skilled jobs they have been trained to fulfil. For example, a migrant providing childcare frees the mother to return to the workforce. Conversely, employing high-skilled migrants in high-skilled jobs allows industries to fill roles where the native labour supply falls short. As the US continues to demonstrate, the flux and mix of cultures leads to innovation. It is now calculated that migrants provide more than half of the innovation in the US, even though they are only around 12 per cent of the population, with Silicon Valley perhaps providing among the most compelling evidence for the beneficial effects of high-skilled migration.

Increasingly, the demographic shift in developed countries to a more aged population will drive these economies to demand an increase in migration in order to maintain a healthy ratio of non-working citizens to working citizens. Demographically, this will only be possible through higher levels of migration. Europe, for example, will require well over 300 million migrants between now and 2050 if it is to maintain its current ratio of workers to dependants. The question is whether popular perceptions of migration will shift to allow what is currently politically impossible. It is not only the developed countries of the West that face this shift. China too faces an ageing population and falling fertility. The coming decades are likely to see increasing global competition for both skilled and less-skilled migrants.

Figure 7 shows the extent to which the workforce in the advanced Organisation for Economic Co-operation and Development

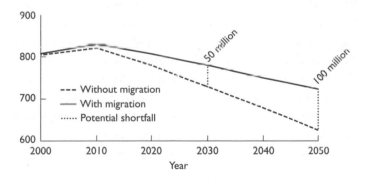

FIGURE 7 Migration potential

Projected population aged 15–64 with and without migration (medium variant) in 'Opening Statement' at *High Level Dialogue on International Migration and Development*, United Nations General Assembly © United Nations, 2006. Reproduced with permission.

(OECD) economies is projected to decline in the coming decades due to demographic pressures, from around 800 million to 600 million people. Even if the number of migrants entering the OECD economies increased by a factor of ten from current levels, they still would only be able to meet half of this employment shortfall.

Sending countries, too, benefit greatly from migration, and despite fears of a 'brain drain', migration is a key channel of growth for developing countries. Those leaving find opportunities in their destination countries that often do not exist in their own. The very fact that economic emigration is possible stimulates people to advance their education—and since they often do not emigrate, and if they do return, this benefits their country directly. The Philippines actively promotes the training of nurses with a view to 'exporting' them to the US and UK, yet the boost this policy has given to the nursing education sector means that the Philippines has 'more trained nurses per capita *at home* than wealthier countries such as Thailand, Malaysia, or the UK'.[27]

Often, what appears to be a 'brain drain' is in fact 'brain circulation', with migrants returning to the sending country years or even decades later, bringing capital, global connections, cutting-edge expertise, and new ideas back with them. The booming Bangalore IT industry is the result of this dynamic. In addition, by sending part of their wage packet home through remittances—to the tune of more than US$372 billion in 2011—migrant workers provide a source of money 'larger than direct foreign investment and more than twice as large as official aid received by developing countries'.[28] More than fifty million people in Latin America and the Caribbean alone are supported by remittances.

The challenge with migration is that despite these extensive and incontrovertible long-term economy-wide gains, host governments and native populations will allow themselves to be swayed by the short-term localized costs. Diversity can bring with it disorientation for both native and migrant, and it is too often only after an initial phase that the richness of the new society is appreciated and a new level of social cohesion achieved. This sense of dislocation in both groups is exacerbated by the perception that the migrants are taking the place of natives in the workplace and straining local services rather than invigorating the economy. Without concerted action on the part of the host government, the migrant group risks being excluded and forming a separate community. Combined with economic hardship, this can turn into a socioeconomic underclass. The danger with migration is not that it will bring something bad, but that governments will not have the foresight to allow it to realize the range of potential benefits.

Orphan issue

At the global level, migration is the orphan of the international system. There is no UN organization for migration. Rather, aspects of migration are dealt with by specific institutions, for example, refugees by the UN High Commission for Refugees (UNHCR). The International Organization for Migration (IOM) has grown in recent decades to perform many global functions, but it does not cover all countries and has no global force of law. In a period of intense globalization, the international laws and institutions governing migration have lagged many decades behind increasing mobility. As in other areas where there is global lawlessness, the strong countries dominate the weak. Their ability to bully is one of the reasons they are not supportive of a more even playing field.

There are areas of migration policy reform that would benefit even the powerful rich nations and which could be relatively uncontroversial. These include areas such as pension portability and the application of minimum wage, safety, health, and environmental standards to migrants, who too often have become an unregulated underclass that undermines domestic standards. Another area where global agreement is likely to suit all parties is with respect to data. There is no common definition or measurement of migration flows, so discussions are hampered from the outset by a failure of common nomenclature.

Climate Change

Rising connectivity, whether financial, physical, human (through travel and migration), or informational, is a key driver of new 'global challenges'. But it is by no means the only one. We will have to contend with a widening set of escalating and increasingly overlapping challenges over the next century—including terrorism, war, nuclear proliferation, and environmental degradation. The solutions to these problems are varied but have key elements in common. If we can solve one, we will also have made major progress towards solving others, for we will have demonstrated to national governments and citizens that global governance works. Cooperation is a learnt activity, and learning how to cooperate requires incremental progress, with success building on prior lessons and experience.

Given the brevity of this book, there is not enough space to cover the many different global challenges. However, there is one additional challenge that we cannot avoid, especially given its high potential for widespread damage and the weakness of the international response. That challenge is anthropogenic (resulting from human activity) global warming.

The likely consequences of continued greenhouse gas emissions are often talked about, but they are worth restating: during the next century, global warming is likely to increase the intensity of droughts, floods, hurricanes, storms, and wildfires, melt the polar ice caps, raise the sea level, and be associated with dramatic changes in cropping patterns and food insecurity. Poor people will suffer most, as famines become more frequent and marginal lands become even less viable. Biodiversity will come under increased threat, with many more species of animal and plant life becoming extinct. Food and water supplies, already under pressure from a burgeoning population, are likely to become even more limited.

The scientific consensus behind anthropogenic global warming is overwhelming. While members of the public still often think that scientists are divided, recent polls suggest that upwards of 98 per cent of scientists with relevant experience in the field endorse the idea that humans are contributing to climate change.[29]

Yet moves to ameliorate global warming have been extremely limited. Multilateral treaties such as the Kyoto Protocol, which made a few steps towards limiting carbon emissions, have been ratified and subsequently ignored by a large number of countries. A few stuttering steps forward were agreed at the December 2011 COP_{17} climate change conference and the June 2012 Rio+20 meetings, but with caveats and carve-outs that mean that even a weak binding agreement will at best be enforced from 2020.

In the area of climate change, the gap between the challenge and action on global governance is particularly stark. World emissions of greenhouse gases took a slight dip following the 2008 recession, but are now steadily increasing once more and are projected to keep rising, as is evident from the Intergovernmental Panel on Climate Change (IPCC) projections in Figure 8. These increases are not being driven by a few rogue states, blithely ignoring their long-term interests: in fact, in virtually all countries emissions continue on an upward trend. Unlike the other challenges considered in this book, the effects of emissions are long-term and effectively irreversible.

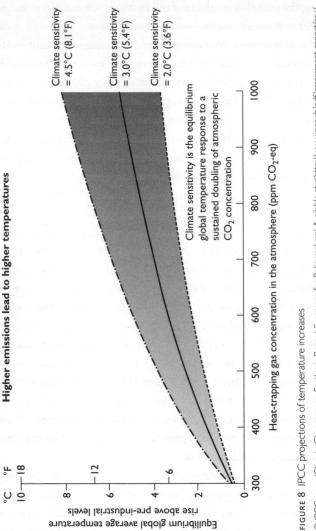

FIGURE 8 IPCC projections of temperature increases

Even if carbon emissions were halted tomorrow, we would still be feeling the cumulative effects of the past 300 years of industrialization for millennia to come.

One of the most concerning aspects of climate change is the uncertainty surrounding the consequences. The few remaining climate sceptics often latch on to this fact—they claim that mitigating action will have concrete costs now, whereas the benefits are mainly conjecture. It might all turn out much better than we think. A breakthrough technology may allow us to vastly reduce emissions overnight, or even to directly counteract climate change by changing the composition of the atmosphere.

Sceptical about sceptics

However, uncertainty cuts both ways. While the situation may turn out better than expected, it may also turn out to be worse. Greenhouse gas emissions have the potential to interact with other developments, amplifying the problems we already face. In addition, in other areas of personal and global activity, uncertainty, when it is associated with a non-trivial risk, is reason enough for global action. There was no certainty of nuclear war, yet treaties were signed to limit the risk; there is no certainty of pandemics, yet we focus on them. There is no certainty of fire in our homes or that our cars or valuables will be stolen, yet we take precautions and invest to further reduce the potential risks. When it comes to climate change most people appear to be unable to make the same sort of risk-based calculations.

Climate change will increase the stress on systems already struggling to cope with growing populations and increased income. Infrastructure in many developing countries, especially access to electricity and water, is already substandard. Increasing migration to places of environmental vulnerability also poses deep challenges for policy makers. According to a recent 'Foresight' report by the UK Government, there may be between 114 and 192 million additional people living in the floodplains in urban areas in Africa and Asia by 2060, compared with 2000.[30]

Climate change brings with it extreme weather events, significantly complicating the already substantial challenge of providing critical societal services such as food and energy. It is highly likely to have a severely negative impact on societies that already suffer the greatest risks to their water supplies. The IPCC concluded that all the areas they had studied had suffered from lower freshwater supplies as a result of global warming. Some of the poorest areas of the world are the most exposed due to their semi-arid climate.[31]

Emergent behaviour

Interactions within the biosphere could also be dangerous. The climate, like the financial sector, is much studied and little understood. It has the potential to manifest 'emergent' behaviour. A multiplicity of simple actions can combine to create unforeseen properties of the system as a whole.

For instance, there is significant concern among climate scientists that we may reach some sort of tipping point. A positive feedback loop may emerge in which global warming changes some other aspect of the climate, which in turn leads to increased global warming. Upon reaching a point such as this, global warming may become severe abruptly. There would be very little time to adapt to the change and the effects could therefore be devastating.

There are several possible ways that positive feedback could occur. For example, higher tundra temperatures may lead to a melting of the permafrost and release vast amounts of trapped greenhouse gases. Warm air is able to hold more moisture than cold air, and water vapour can act as a powerful greenhouse gas. As the oceans warm they will release carbon dioxide that will further amplify warming. Land and water are less reflective than ice, so melting ice is likely to create a feedback loop. Any one of these mechanisms, or a combination of these few examples out of the long list of potential tipping points, could create a crisis with devastating impacts for hundreds of millions of people. They urgently require global interventions. No one country can possibly deal with climate change—it requires concerted action at the global level.

Global Problems in the 21st Century

Connectivity does not just aid the spread of pathogens. It also allows us to react quickly and decisively in the face of natural disasters. Within twenty-four hours of the 2010 earthquake in Haiti, personnel, medicine, and materials were arriving in Port-au-Prince. The speed of this response is impressive in itself—but even more impressive given that the first search and rescue team to arrive had been dispatched from Iceland, almost 4,000 miles from Haiti.[32] They were closely followed by a Chinese team, who had travelled more than 8,000 miles.[33] Help arrived from across the world. Global responses on this scale would have been impossible just a few decades ago.

The great challenge of all these global problems is that they are extraordinarily hard to predict. Any emerging pathogen worth worrying about will be unlike those that we have seen before. Any emerging financial crisis will have unique features that prevent regulators from spotting the danger of systemic collapse. The cyber capacity to cripple technology systems in countries and companies grows more innovative and advanced each day. When it comes to migration, we may appreciate that in theory it brings benefits, but we are reluctant to deal with the consequences in terms of the stresses and strains it places on our local communities and societies. Climate change meanwhile is too complex and unpredictable, and the measures required in terms of decarbonization of our energy, transport, and food systems too radical for virtually anyone to comprehend, let alone to act on. All these looming challenges require visionary leadership to comprehend and manage. Future chapters consider how this may be found.

In this chapter I have briefly outlined five different classes of 21st-century challenges: financial crisis, pandemic, cybersecurity, migration, and climate change. Underpinned by increasing connectivity and interdependencies, all of these problems are likely to become more urgent in coming years.

There is no sign of a retreat from our hyper-connected world. Nor should there be. I have emphasized that there are real gains to be made from growing networks. Global population increases, income growth, education, urbanization, and technological advances will mean that more people will be able to benefit from connections and networks than ever before.

It also means that there are more potential dangers in the world, producing more greenhouse gases and with a greater demand for energy, transport, and manufactured goods. As the complex networks grow they will not only facilitate the movement of ideas, people, money, and information, but the spread of contagion and cascading systemic risk. The speed and scope of these changes requires a fundamental rethink of the way we approach governance.

CHAPTER 2

Reconciling Global, National, and Local Interests

When Local and Global Collide

Concerns about financial stability, pandemics, security, migration, and the environment are not new in themselves. We have accounts of the destructive power of pathogens dating back to well before Ancient Greece and the 'plague of Athens'. Crime has doubtless existed since the creation of laws to be broken. Speculative fevers have been driving asset bubbles for centuries—the 'tulip mania' of the Netherlands in the 17th century is a prominent example of an early asset market collapse. Government action on pollution dates back to at least King Edward I, who banned the burning of sea-coal in 1272.

These problems have historically been dealt with domestically. National governments and rulers have produced laws and regulations to protect their populations. When national policies could not deal with issues, rules were sought to find global or at least regional solutions. Examples date back to the earliest peace treaties, including the agreement between the Egyptian and Hittite kingdoms in 1274 BCE and centuries later the Treaty of Paris (1815) and Treaty of Versailles (1919).

For the most part, prior to the 20th century, agreements tended to be regional in nature and reflect the resolution of clashes of imperial and commercial ambitions. The failure to deal effectively with these issues is regarded by many historians to have given rise to the deepening structural weaknesses that culminated in the First and Second World Wars.

Increased interconnectivity and economic growth have changed the demands placed on global governance. The challenges of the global commons increasingly render domestic solutions inadequate. The orthodox definition of global commons refers to natural assets that are outside national jurisdiction, such as the oceans, outer space, and the Antarctic. My use of the term goes back to the usage in old English law, where the common was a tract of land shared by the residents of the village, but belonging to no individual as it was held in common for the good of all. The Internet and cyberspace are in this respect a global commons, as is peace and security. The tragedy of the commons refers to the overexploitation of common resources, originally typically by herders, as no single person had the motivation or responsibility to limit the number or extent of the grazing of livestock and so the resource collapsed. Many of the challenges of global governance are rooted in the tragedy of the commons, in that no one country feels motivated to make sacrifices or circumscribe their behaviour for the common good.

In this chapter, I investigate the existing global institutions and their capacity to tackle key questions of global governance. I also look briefly at regional structures and other global groupings already in place in search of alternative mechanisms that might serve to mobilize action for global change.

Wherever possible, domestic solutions are preferable. Domestic institutions tend to date back much further than global governance structures, and are generally accepted by citizens as a legitimate source of binding law. Embedded common values and culture ensure that interests are more unified, and laws that have been produced can be enforced through the national legislation and judiciary. Social norms can also act as a more effective enforcement mechanism: social pressure can regulate individual behaviour.

International institutions, such as the UN or the WTO, are more remote. States and citizens see them as intruding on their sovereignty. Thousands of international treaties have been created, but too many are barely worth the paper they are written on. Some, like the Kyoto Protocol, are simply ignored by countries that wish to avoid their implications. To the extent that enforcement mechanisms are available, they are typically ineffective as they are not compatible with domestic political processes. Local regulatory systems take precedence in local politics and administration. Where the implementation of a treaty or international agreement requires legislative or other changes at the national level, it is held hostage to domestic politics.

One may conclude from this that it would be best to simply rely on national politics and domestic political decisions. However, the challenges described in Chapter 1 cannot be solved at the domestic level alone. The cross-border or spillover impacts mean that without global solutions national management of the issue is severely compromised. States will be unable unilaterally to prevent these problems from adversely affecting their citizens. Cooperation is thus an imperative. Despite the difficulties, we need to find ways to build a bridge between national and global concerns.

In the second half of the 20th century there was some success in this. Growing interdependence and the threat of war did lead to some progress, not least in that we have avoided another tragic world war. What lessons can be drawn from this?

Local Rules

The complexities and difficulties of global governance mean that global problem-solving should be restricted to those issues where this is an absolute requirement. Global governance should be confined to areas where only global cooperation will enable states to effectively deal with the problems at hand. Where other options have been exhausted it becomes essential to overcome the inefficacy of the global governance regime. Even in these situations, nation states should continue to play a key role. Without a national capacity to implement global solutions these will remain vacuous and cannot be implemented. Nation states are thus both the primary source of help as well as the likely obstacle to the achievement of effective global governance. Global institutions and actions are the last resort.

Climate change provides an illustrative example of the balance between national and global power and capability. Each individual state has only a limited ability to decrease the incidence of climate change—even if they cut their own emissions to zero, they will still be affected by the emissions of other countries. There are two notable exceptions. Both China and the US produce such a large slice of global emissions that stringent regulation could make a qualitative difference to the effects of climate change on their populations.[34] Also, mitigating measures enacted unilaterally (for instance, the increased use of crops that are resilient to changes in climate) could be important.[35] However, these measures cannot replace the need for international cooperation—they can do little to prevent the loss of biodiversity or, over the long-term, broader impacts on the global climate such as the displacement of individuals due to rising sea levels or changes in farming potential.

United We Stand, Divided We Fall

States acting independently to limit their exposure to pandemics similarly are unable to create the protection that could be afforded by international cooperation. There is some parallel to the climate change problem: extensive transport and travel networks have created a situation in which no individual country can control risk unilaterally. An outbreak in other states, if mismanaged, will spread quickly. Short of preventing all movement across its borders, or screening and placing under quarantine all individuals who attempt to enter, a single government can do little to prevent exposure to pandemics. These measures are generally prohibitively costly and unsustainable during a prolonged outbreak and would not function for airborne pandemics, such as those transmitted by birds.

This is not to say that domestic preparations can have no effect. However, effective action is reliant on international cooperation. In the case of pandemics, the most important aspect is information sharing. Crafting an effective domestic response requires knowledge of the biological properties of the pathogen, its response to various drugs and vaccines, as well as its epidemiological characteristics. Knowing where the pathogen has become prevalent allows for targeted screening of individuals travelling from those locations. Understanding how the disease is transmitted makes it possible to reduce contagion.

The insufficiency of a domestic response extends beyond information problems. Connectivity means that the inadequacy of infrastructure internationally can severely limit the ability of each country to deal with domestic risk. Many states have governments that perform basic functions but lack the infrastructure and staff to perform the short-term preventative measures necessary to prevent cascading systemic crises. In the case of a pandemic, this requires identifying the outbreak of a novel pathogen, distributing information, administering vaccinations, and other measures which reflect a level of preparedness and capability which not all, or even most, countries share.

The extent to which countries share scarce resources during crises can also have a critical impact on the evolution of the threat. For example, new mathematical models suggest that it would be beneficial for two interconnected neighbouring countries to pool their resources to arrest and isolate a pandemic. In some cases, directing resources to one's neighbour could even be more beneficial than pursuing domestic vaccinations that would fall well short of targets.[36]

Contagion across borders is not restricted to pandemics. It is a characteristic of a growing number of systemic risks and reflects the underside of globalization and hyper-connectivity. Where risks are not contained at the national level, risk management has to be considered at the regional or global level.

We highlighted in Chapter 1 that the Internet is a shared global resource and that cybercriminality is a common threat that requires global as well as national action. One cannot fight criminals who transcend national borders with justice systems that are constrained by national jurisdictions.

A common response is that there should be increased monitoring of Internet activity by Internet service providers (ISPs), allowing the identification and isolation of the zombie computers that they host. Such a solution would be ineffective if implemented in a single state—ISPs would only be able to monitor the Internet activity of their customers, who would represent a small fraction of the possible sources of malicious code and cybercrime.

Reducing cybercrime not only relies on policies implemented at the systemic level, but will also gain from the cohesive design of those policies. For instance, international prosecution for cybercrime would be significantly easier if the definitions of cybercrime were shared among states. Cyberaggression calls for a similar response—disincentives cannot be put into place unless an international legal framework is established. States will be able to encourage aggression without fear of retribution, knowing that they can easily block investigations. Individuals residing in uncooperative states will know that their destructive acts carry little personal risk. As Estonia found in 2007, domestic enthusiasm for prosecution will be ineffective without international cooperation.

While the crimes committed are not in themselves new—cybercriminals practise fraud, theft, blackmail, and industrial espionage—when crime moves onto the Internet sovereign states become increasingly unable to enforce the law. Finding the perpetrators behind a cyberattack is difficult in itself. There are many different ways for a criminal to hide their identity: connections are often routed through many different countries and attacks can use captured computers belonging to unsuspecting individuals across the world.

Even if the criminal is found, ensuring that they are brought to justice can be exceptionally difficult. Often they are based in countries without strong legal systems. For instance, early viruses often originated in the Philippines which, at the time, had no cybercrime legislation. Extradition is often prohibitively costly.

These arguments extend to financial stability. Parallel to pathogens, financial crises spread abroad via a contagion effect. As we saw following the 2008 financial crisis, the exposure to damage is not a simple product of domestic measures—even countries with only tangential connections to the subprime market have suffered severe economic losses.

For these reasons, limiting the risk of financial crises is not as simple as enacting good legislation at home, especially in a world where capital (both physical and human) is increasingly mobile. Restricting the destructive capabilities of financial institutions in the US may only serve to push these institutions and practices abroad if attempted unilaterally. Policy needs to be determined and enforced at the global level if it is to have the desired effect.

Another parallel to pathogens is the importance of information sharing. This is key in the context of an innovative and fast-moving financial sector. Regulators need to have a full understanding of the global financial market in order to understand the exposure to systemic risk. As with pathogens, domestic measures will be ineffective unless they are devised in an international context.

Misaligned Incentives

There are, however, plenty of areas in which bilateral, regional, or even international cooperation is necessary and successful, such as the global postal system or international air traffic control. Most people do not lie awake at night, even when flying, worrying about the rules that govern air traffic. This is because all countries have a vested interest in assuring safe air traffic, and countries that refuse to cooperate can be boycotted by international airlines.

The new challenges we have outlined are different in their degrees of complexity in securing a solution and the varying interests of key countries. Aspects of these new challenges make cooperation between states particularly difficult or ineffective.

The risks posed by finance, cybersecurity, and pandemics are evolving extremely rapidly. They reflect the exponential growth in the density of physical and virtual connections engendered by globalization and technological change. The nature of the cybersecurity challenge changes almost daily, as new technologies are developed and new weaknesses in the system uncovered. Viruses used to be spread by floppy disk. Now they can spread through file-sharing software and email. It has only become obvious over the last two years that viruses targeting industrial control systems and built into the hardware and software could become a real danger. Cooperation itself is not sufficient if it is not designed for accelerated evolution. We need fast and fluid cooperation, able to adapt to changing circumstances. As we will see below, the traditional international treaty system is poorly suited to provide this flexibility.

In finance, the development of new instruments and the increase in the speed of trading and the distribution of products follow Moore's Law, which is depicted in Figure 9. The power of computer-enabled products and processes is doubling in speed, for the same price, at least every two years. The salaries paid to the mathematicians and physicists who are drawn into the development of these products are multiples of those of the alternative professions awaiting the brightest graduates. No wonder the regulators and supervisors are falling increasingly behind and the public's and politicians' understanding of the issues is depleted to a dismal state.

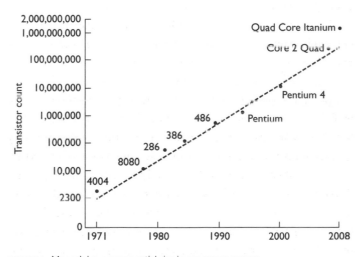

FIGURE 9 Moore's Law: exponential rise in processor power

Transistor counts for integrated circuits plotted against their dates of introduction
Antranik.org

Similar dynamics drive the threat of pandemics. Dangerous pandemics will spread through unusual vectors, or will be resistant to normal treatments. Timing is of the utmost importance—it is much easier and cheaper to limit the spread of a pandemic in the earlier stages of an outbreak. Cooperation needs to be timely to be effective. Meanwhile, the development of bio-pathogens, built using DNA synthesizers, means that the technological race to prevent new forms of risk spread by viruses created by design or accident is reaching altogether new proportions. Again, the capability of governance systems is lagging behind at an alarming rate.

The ability to protect against these risks depends on the capabilities of states. Many states lack the ability to detect and control an outbreak, or to track down and prosecute a cybercriminal, or to identify the critical nodes in finance, just as they do not have the means to identify and isolate a potential pandemic at source. In these cases, funding and technical skills must come from the more developed countries or an international agency.

Can We Cooperate?

Unfortunately, it is much easier to recognize that this funding must be provided than to determine who should provide it and how it should be deployed. Each developed country has an incentive to play down their ability or desire to pay, so that they can benefit from the increased protection without bearing the costs. The result is too little cooperation.

Even the wealthiest countries, with the greatest numbers of skilled professionals and institutional capacity, do not have the means to manage systemic risks on their own. If there is one lesson from the financial crisis, it is this.

There is an additional issue in cyberaggression and climate change. It is likely that some countries believe that they have little to gain from cooperation. In the case of cyberaggression, a country may believe that both its defensive and offensive cyber capabilities are far more developed than in other countries. Examples could include China, or the US. Unfortunately, this is likely to obstruct international efforts to limit cyberaggression. It is also based on a particularly short-sighted conception of the benefits from cooperation. The 'aggressors' in cyberspace are not just states, but also individuals and groups. By shunning cooperation, states may increase their ability to attack and spy upon other states, but they also leave themselves open to attacks from myriad state and non-state actors.

With regard to the issue of climate change, some countries may feel that they may actually benefit. This is particularly the case for countries in the far north, bordering the Arctic Circle. They may consider that the potential benefits from new oil and other exploration and from increases in agricultural yields as their weather becomes milder outweigh the costs of mitigation and global cooperation.

Within climate change and financial stability, as with cyberaggression, lack of cooperation is the result of misaligned incentives as well as, for some countries, resource and capacity constraints.

Political Realities

The democratic imperative may compound the difficulties associated with global governance. Within democratic politics parties often rely on funding from wealthy individuals, organizations, and industry or sector associations. Lobby groups work to ensure that regulations and actions advance their members' interests and that any actions that may impose a burden are opposed. In climate change and financial stability, powerful lobby groups representing private interests can influence government via their hold on the purse strings of political campaigns as well as indirectly through funding media and other activities.

The problem is exacerbated by the uncertainty surrounding potentially devastating, unpredictable, and highly complex challenges. A government that knew financial breakdown was imminent unless it imposed regulation wouldn't be too concerned about annoying some bankers. Unfortunately, governments never know when or where a financial crisis will strike. They similarly are unsure about the likelihood and impact of threats from pandemics. There is therefore an incentive for governments that have a short-term political horizon, to 'take your chances'. Similar myopic imperatives also hold for climate change: the consequences of further emissions are obscure, and there is no clear causal link between any particular natural disaster and a government's refusal to limit emissions. In migration the short-term costs to local communities can overwhelm the society-wide and longer-term benefits. Where there is a trade-off in terms of budgets or regulations, democracy adds to the pressure for short-term and local preferences to be favoured over longer-term and global problem-solving.

Many preventative measures inflict pain today with the hope of gain tomorrow. Such policies can be unpopular. Individuals who fail to take the future benefits into account may punish the government now, and the benefits of the policy may only accrue long after the current government has been defeated. The opposite is also common—governments enact policies that cause long-term damage to the interests of the citizenry but offer short-term gains. Many economists have claimed that the expansion of homeownership by the Bush administrations took this form.[37] Increasing access to credit among the poor was popular and allowed them to scale up consumption, but it led to frailties in the financial system that culminated in the subprime crisis.

If incentives are misaligned in this way, there is little reason to expect domestic governments acting individually to take significant action on global problems such as climate change or financial stability.

Coordinating Migration

Incentives are similarly misaligned in the case of migration. Setting aside the UNHCR, which deals specifically with refugees, there is currently no UN agency responsible for global migration or indeed another organization on the model of the WTO, IMF, or World Bank. An inadequate system of rules can at least be targeted for reform, but migration, like climate change, lacks any global system of rules at all. As a result, migration policy is left to the whim of largely uncoordinated national governments. Just as climate change policy is prey to lobbying from corporate interests, national migration policy is prone to influence from the short-term and local fears of citizens. As the Global Commission on International Migration reported in 2005, 'In some parts of the world, negative attitudes towards migrants persist, despite the fact that entire sectors of the economy depend on foreign labour'.[38] The result is a coordination failure equivalent to economic protectionism as everyone responds only to their own local situation.

For over 100,000 years, migration has provided the means for mankind to escape poverty, conflict, and natural disasters. The era of accelerated globalization since 1990 has ironically been associated with the proliferation of nation states and increasingly stringent border controls. People increasingly are trapped in geographies that for a variety of interrelated factors cannot sustain them. The situation will become even more complicated with the onset of climate change. The former President of the Maldives, Mohamed Nasheed, once mooted his government's interest in buying land in India, Sri Lanka, or Australia to relocate some of the Maldives population as their islands become progressively uninhabitable as oceans rise due to climate change.[39] With environmental displacement expected around the world, the case for coordinated migration policy, not least for the poorest environmental refugees, becomes even more pressing.

Countries such as those of the European Union and Japan, as well as China and a number of other emerging markets, face rapidly aging populations which will lead to growing competition for skilled people. As a result, we face the complex situation of a possible race to the bottom in terms of states' demands from skilled migrant workers and a simultaneous shortage of opportunities for less-skilled people who may have greater need to escape poverty and find employment. The danger is a two-tier system in which the skilled move freely across the world and let states woo them with competing offers, while the unskilled are left to suffer the consequences of dire poverty and environmental and other natural and human-induced pressures. In order to avoid the perverse effects of each of these scenarios states would be better off, and migrants protected, by a shared framework for migration.

The International Organization for Migration has no globally agreed mandate to assist migrants, as states set their policies individually in this important area. Most states have not even signed the UN Convention on the Rights of Migrant Workers and Members of Their Families, which would provide some standard by which to call their policies into question.[40] In 2005, the Global Commission on International Migration (GCIM) delivered its final report to

UN Secretary-General Kofi Annan, in which it called for a new international regime to govern cross-border flows of migrants.[41] Subsequently, key governments and even the differing UN agencies with an interest in migration could not agree to cede control. The Global Migration Forum for Development and a discussion group among UN agencies working on migration were all that the process could yield. As a result, there is no global legally binding forum in which states and interest groups can add items to an agenda for discussion and action. A globally agreed set of definitions of migration to aid data collection and comparison has not even been achieved. This demonstrates just how difficult cooperation is on this politically vexed issue.

Transparency and Free Riding

There are some cases in which coordination can be relatively painless. It is instructive to return to the example of international air traffic control. It seems obvious to all the participants that cooperation is necessary—a system in which each country determines their regulations independently would create chaos. The act of coordination itself is generally not that costly, and the benefits for each country far outweigh the costs. Most importantly, no country has any reason to defect from this system once it is in place. To do so would only cause widespread confusion while conferring no benefits on the deviator.

Coordination in financial policy can sometimes look like this. Consider, for instance, transparency requirements. The lack of transparency in the shadow banking sector is often cited as a major failure of financial services regulation, but attempting to impose transparency unilaterally can be extremely difficult.[42] Firms can play states against one another by threatening to move their business if they are forced to comply with onerous standards. As argued above, contagion means that the likely benefit of unilateral regulation is small. Firms that do not want to be monitored can move overseas, and unless the state is willing to cut off financial connectivity they will still be exposed to the risk they create. Coordination is necessary to fill the gap. If standards of transparency are agreed internationally and imposed simultaneously, regulatory 'shopping around' becomes impossible. What's more, once transparency requirements are in place, states have little individual incentive to abolish them. The likely result of withdrawing the requirements would be an inward flood of shady operators, destabilizing the national financial sector.

Transparency requirements clearly need to be tackled through cooperation. Reaching international agreements can be tricky, to say the least, especially as the financial sector is a powerful private interest in some states. Once agreements are reached, they are most effective where they are self-enforcing as all parties have an interest in ensuring the continuation of the system.

Unfortunately, this is not the case with climate change, as countries have an incentive to be free riders and to avoid reducing emissions, so long as they feel that others will make reductions. A coordinated response is still necessary if we are to deal with global warming, but each country faces sizable incentives to deviate from the agreement at the first opportunity.

This is known in economics as the 'free-rider' problem. The problem is that emissions affect every country, regardless of where they are emitted. As argued above, reductions in the emissions of any one country will make a relatively small difference to domestic exposure to global warming, with the exception of a couple of large emitters. Even the third largest emitter, India, only releases around 5 per cent of the annual global carbon dioxide emissions. For the United Kingdom, the number is even lower—under 2 per cent.[43]

While the UK would gain from a worldwide reduction in emissions, it can achieve very little on its own.

Imagine that an agreement is reached among all large economies to reduce emissions by 10 per cent. If all other countries comply, the UK is set to gain substantially. Extreme weather events would be less likely than if action wasn't taken, and sea levels would be lower than in a business-as-usual scenario. The influential UK Report on the economics of climate change by Lord Nicholas Stern estimated that the benefits of emission reduction outweigh the costs ten to one.[44]

But given that all other countries are cooperating, is there any reason for the UK to do so as well? A thought experiment shows why it is difficult for countries to commit and demonstrates the erosive power of the free-rider problem. For example, if the UK does not reduce emissions it would still enjoy almost all the benefits of reduced global warming while being able to avoid the costs that cutting emissions would have involved. This is the reason that some people feel they might as well carry on as normal.

What if the other countries reason the same way? In this case, reducing emissions in the UK would still be costly, but would confer almost no benefits. Again, the best course of action could be to carry on as normal.

So either way, the government in the UK has some incentive to defect from the agreement. However, if other governments adopt the same line of reasoning, emissions would carry on increasing. This occurs even though every country would be individually better off if all countries reduced their emissions. The general solution to free-rider problems is international agreement which binds signatory governments.

At the national level, similar free-riding problems would apply if we tried to fund national defence through voluntary individual contributions. We can't prevent any individual living in a country from benefitting from police or national defence. If a marauding gang is valiantly fought back before they reach my home in Oxford then I will benefit greatly. But so does my neighbour. If we tried to collect voluntary contributions for the police, I would know that how much I donated would make little or no difference as to whether the gang was defeated. The best strategy would appear to be for me to keep my money.

Since almost everyone would be liable to think like me, the police would likely be somewhere in between—underfunded and non-existent. This is why donations to the police are not voluntary. Instead, they are collected in the form of taxes, and paying your taxes is mandatory for everyone resident in the country. Taxes are enforced using the executive power of government—namely, the executive power to punish noncompliance with fines and jail sentences. The result is that everyone is better off.

There is no equivalent institution at the international level. Treaties can produce agreements that legally forbid nations from certain actions, but there is often no ability to enforce compliance. Resolutions can be ignored with little threat of retribution. Even if they were enforceable, signing up to a treaty is a voluntary act.

This line of thought suggests a possible solution to international free riding. If we created a multilateral institution with powers similar to a national government then we could solve incentive problems. Specifically, this body could have the executive power necessary to force countries to comply. A world government could also solve many of the other problems mentioned above: it would be able to redistribute resources between countries to create capacity, streamline communication, and solve coordination problems by setting international regulatory standards.

There are, however, equally strong reasons to oppose worldwide executive power. So far we have avoided the question of how decision making within such a body would work. It is possible to imagine a democratic legislature drawing representatives from across the world. This is the model used within the European Union (EU): decisions are made within the European Parliament, and members are elected to the European Parliament directly by European citizens.

Legitimacy and Efficacy

Decisions made by a body such as the EU will be caught between the demands of efficacy and legitimacy. The more consensual the decision-making procedure, the more legitimate the outcomes will appear, but the less likely we are to reach agreement. For instance, if we relied on unanimous consent then there would be little point in creating the body in the first place—very little legislation would be produced. Each country would be able to hold out for concessions to benefit their citizens. If we set a lower barrier, such as approval by a simple majority of members, decisions would be more likely to make it through the global legislature, but would also appear less legitimate. Tyranny of the majority would be a serious problem— decisions would invariably benefit some countries more than others, and this would lead to conflict. The quest for efficacy would undermine legitimacy.

The sort of stalemate that can be created by giving competing countries veto power was evident in the UN Security Council over the Cold War period, when both the USSR and the US held a veto. More Security Council resolutions have been reached between 2002 and 2011 than over the entire forty-year period between 1950 and 1990.[45] The July 2012 Russian veto of a Security Council resolution on Syria, despite the atrocities committed against civilians, indicates that this body can still be prone to paralysis at crucial moments. Reform of the UN Security Council is among the many urgent and yet apparently intractable requirements for effective governance in the 21st century.

Legitimacy and effectiveness are intertwined—each affects the other. However, it is important to emphasize that their competing demands are not always zero sum. In the example given above, the lack of legitimacy may feed back into opposition to the institutions enforcing the agreement. Lack of legitimacy can therefore create inefficacy.

Equally, efficacy can create legitimacy. Few people have taken time to understand the process that determines international air traffic regulations. Whatever the process is, it seems to work. The fact that it works creates its own type of legitimacy. The institutions are justified by their results, regardless of the process. The allocation of international Internet names through the Internet Corporation for Assigned Names and Numbers organization has been seen as effective, and therefore legitimate, even though it is a small private foundation with no global accountability.

The direct extension of executive powers to the international level is unlikely to be a solution to any of the challenges we have identified, regardless of how attractive it may seem to some. Health care, security, finance, and carbon emissions are too central to the interests of states. Delegation of power would only be acceptable to states if decisions left significant room for the promotion of state-specific interests—for instance, through the use of highly consensual decision-making procedures. But highly consensual decisions will be unlikely to promote efficiency. The rapid increase in the number of countries, as depicted in Figure 10, makes these problems even more difficult to resolve.

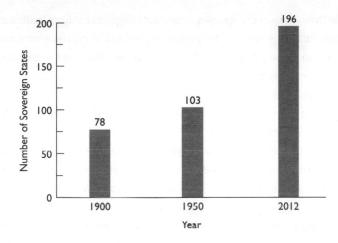

FIGURE 10 Number of countries 1900–2012
Author's own

Many states have suffered from rule by external powers previously, and ex-colonies would be unlikely to welcome foreign intervention and would object to significant delegation. For African and
Latin American countries, the memories of colonial rule are relatively recent and particularly raw, as are those of countries that until
the 1990s were under the Soviet yoke. Recently independent countries are not only particularly reluctant to give up their hard-won
right to national self-determination, but at times are keen to use
international forums to remind their former masters of their legacy.
Forging international consensus requires an overcoming of deep-
rooted suspicions and historical animosity. This requires either
generations of time—which we do not have—or courageous leaders who can rise to the new challenges.

The domination of modern multilaterals, such as the World Bank
and the IMF, by the US, EU, and Japan reinforces suspicions regarding their lack of alignment with the interests of the developing

countries. In order to improve their legitimacy, fundamental improvements in the representation of developing countries are demanded within the boards and decision-making processes of these institutions.

The tension between legitimacy and efficiency is an important one. One way to understand the development of multilateral institutions in the post-war period is as an attempt to strike a balance between the different horns of this dilemma. The institutions were designed to be effective enough to deal with international problems of war, peace, and economic stability. On the other hand, they sought to preserve as much space for self-determination as possible, and create a legitimate forum for decision making.

I argue that while these institutions may have had some success in dealing with 20th-century problems, they have not been able to adapt to the new global challenges that face us today.

The EU represents a striking exception to the unwillingness of countries to cede sovereignty. In areas that many nations regard as sacrosanct—including security, migration, foreign affairs, finance, and carbon emissions—a core of European countries have given up sovereignty. Despite the major difficulties, this has proved sustainable and the trend is to yielding more power, not less, to the European Parliament, European Commission, and associated bodies, such as the European Court of Justice. The recent financial crisis placed a severe strain on these arrangements, but the outcome—which has been to reinforce the powers vested in the Commission—demonstrates the robustness of the system.

Clearly, as the EU has demonstrated, countries are prepared to cede a wide range of power, if not to global structures, at least to supranational regional institutions. What lessons may we draw from this for global governance? This is a topic to which we return below. First, however, it is useful to understand some basic facts about the structure and purpose of the main global governance institutions in place today.

The Existing Institutions

The United Nations

A relatively small set of institutions has dominated the international scene over the past sixty years, all created shortly after the Second World War. Their objectives are distinct, but interlinked. The UN was created in 1945 as a replacement for the League of Nations. The UN was intended to promote peace between nations, and to create a forum for negotiation between states. The structure is complex, but the General Assembly and the Security Council are the central organs. The General Assembly is formally the heart of the UN, a quasi-legislature with one member representing each state. It is charged with appointing non-permanent members of the Security Council, overseeing the budget, and can produce non-binding resolutions by vote.

The Security Council has more power—particularly the ability to produce resolutions on matters of war and peace that are legally binding for all members of the UN. It is comprised of fifteen members, of which five are permanent and possess the power to veto any resolution (China, France, Russia, the UK, and the US). Assuming that a resolution is not vetoed, it requires a nine-vote majority to pass. The UN includes over twenty quasi-independent agencies and funds, including the WHO, the Food and Agricultural Organization (FAO), UN Human Rights Council (UNHRC), and the UN Development Programme (UNDP).

The structure of these organizations varies, but they tend to have several features in common. First, membership is voluntary, and accordingly they tend to have a smaller number of members than the UN General Assembly. The agencies are designed to address specific issues with, in theory, clearly delineated responsibilities. Often they were established to enable cooperation in highly technical areas—international postal systems or air traffic control, for instance. Third, though some regularly produce binding agreements, they only ever bind the organization's members, not the wider membership of the UN. Fourth, there is significant variation in their financing structure. Some are financed almost entirely by subscriptions from their members. Others rely almost entirely on contributions from other bodies, such as charities. Many receive substantial support from the state in which they are based.

Together, these agencies represent a spaghetti bowl of overlapping mandates. Once established, they tend to develop a momentum of their own, and only one has been shut down. Agencies created for one reason are adapted to fill new niches—the International Labour Organization, for instance, has become progressively more involved in work on globalization over its lifetime. In many cases the mandates have sprawled in a number of directions to address new issues or various key donors' changing interests.

An additional problem is that the UN aspires in its staffing to reflect the range of its shareholders, offering what for many nationals are relatively lucrative and secure contracts, leading to low employment turnover and rapid ageing of skills. With funding increasingly directed to specific donor-led projects, the institutions have found it difficult to respond to existing problems, let alone the looming issues. With a number of global institutions captured by donor governments and by staff, there is understandable reluctance to create new agencies. Meanwhile, the reform of the UN remains a perennial topic. Numerous committees and expert groups have sought to streamline and improve the effectiveness of the UN and its agencies. Unfortunately, while their reports remain ignored, governments bicker over the smallest of reforms. Having spent many months of my life engaged in these activities, I can attest to the frustration of both the participants and observers as even apparently minor obstacles to reform become intractable.

Bretton Woods institutions

The World Bank's core directive is the alleviation of poverty and the IMF's is exchange rate stability—although their mandates have mushroomed to include everything from financial regulation to the promotion of clean air.

The two Bretton Woods institutions have a similar structure. At the top is a Board of Governors that includes ministerial-level representatives from every member country. Each member has a certain voting power, determined by a formula that takes into account some combination of historic GDP, international reserves, and past contributions to the institution. The Board of Governors meets once per year, and votes on the admittance of new members and changes to institutional structure. Most of the powers of the Governors are delegated to an Executive Board, which consists of five members representing the founding countries (the US, the UK, Japan, France, and Germany) and nineteen (the IMF) or twenty (the World Bank) other members, most of whom represent constituencies of countries. The Executive Board appoints and is chaired by the head of management—the President of the World Bank or the Managing Director of the IMF—and is charged with oversight. The Board also makes the most significant operational and strategic decisions.

Evolution not revolution

The structure of these institutions has changed little since their inception. The main difference is that they now have many more members—the UN has grown from fifty-one member states in 1946 to 193 member states in 2012.[46] This increase has been driven by the ascension of originally reluctant states, the opening up of membership to a larger number of states (originally limited to those countries that had declared war on at least one Axis power), and the proliferation of nation states around the world. This is mainly the result of decolonization, and the break-up of the Soviet Union. In reaction to increased membership, more seats have been added to the Security Council, as well as to the Executive Boards of the IMF and the World Bank. Voting shares have also been reformed slightly in the latter organizations. But, for the most part, the formal decision-making architecture has stayed the same and the old G7 nations (France, Germany, Italy, Japan, the UK, the US, and Canada) constitute an effective majority on both boards.

The structures of the UN and Bretton Woods institutions largely represent the constellation of international power sixty years ago. The permanent members of the Security Council are no longer the only major military powers—Japan spends almost as much on its military as Russia and the UK, yet has a fraction of their voting power. The US, the EU, and Japan represent almost 54 per cent of voting power in the IMF and World Bank Board of Governors.[47]

The UN and the Bretton Woods institutions can take some of the credit for the relative peace and progress in poverty reduction over the past sixty years. After all, we are yet to experience another conflict on the scale of the Second World War, despite decades of tension between competing, heavily armed superpowers. Perhaps the presence of nuclear weapons and the prospect of 'mutually assured destruction' have been sufficient to discourage large-scale conflict, the Security Council of the UN has also played a role.

Despite numerous crises, it is only recently that the world has experienced anything approaching the severity of the Great

Depression. The World Bank and the IMF can take a small share of the credit for the decades of global financial stability and the achievements in poverty reduction and growth in the post-Second World War period.

The terrible irony is that whereas the policies adopted by the Bretton Woods institutions have served many (but certainly not all) developing countries well, and to a significant extent reflect the orthodox macroeconomic approaches developed in the advanced countries, the advanced countries themselves failed to heed the lessons that they promoted with great vigour around the world. Much of the damage caused during the financial crisis was a result of developed countries not practising what they preached. As a result, many advanced economies are now experiencing severe adjustment policies not unlike those which developing countries were forced to endure in the 1970s and 1980s. Then, as now, criticism was voiced against overly simplistic and self-defeating austerity policies and arguments made for the need to focus on sustainable growth and employment.

One should not exaggerate the role of the IMF and World Bank, since the greatest global achievements, not least in China and India, have resulted from independent economic strategies which cannot be attributed to the Bretton Woods institutions. In addition, even if on aggregate they have contributed positively, development history is littered with terrible mistakes and setbacks occasioned by misguided advice from the too-dominant institutions. Whereas the UN is seen by many as legitimate at the cost of effectiveness, the Bretton Woods institutions have the opposite problem—they may be seen as effective but often not seen to be legitimate.

The World Trade Organization

The WTO focuses on the establishment of a rules-based trading system. Established in 1995, it is one of the youngest international organizations, and evolved out of the General Agreement on Tariffs and Trade (GATT). The GATT, formed in 1944, was designed to complement the IMF and World Bank in promoting international economic cooperation. It undertook a series of negotiating rounds to tackle trade barriers, although without full consent from its entire membership these agreements were considered to be only codes for action. To keep up with a globalizing economy, the GATT was given organizational muscle and permanency through the creation of the WTO. The remit was expanded beyond trade in agriculture and manufactures, to include trade in services, intellectual property, and trade facilitation.

The WTO functions as a forum for negotiation between states on trade disputes and to oversee the implementation of agreements. A succession of trade negotiations have, over the past sixty years, sought to establish a more even rules-based system for international trade, with each round named after the city or country in which the negotiations were initiated. The current Doha round of negotiations aims to extend the benefits of globalization to developing countries by cutting agricultural subsidies and barriers to trade. It has been under way since 2001 and yet agreement has still not been reached. While the round aims to advance some core developing-country interests (it has also been labelled 'the development round'), the fact that it has been unable to escape the gridlock in global governance means that many countries are now resorting to bilateral and regional arrangements which fall well short of the benefits arising from multilateralism.

Whereas the leaders of the IMF and World Bank are appointed by the Europeans and the US, respectively, the Director General of the WTO is elected. Membership of the WTO requires that countries agree to abide by the rules of the organization which are differentiated according to level of development, with the poorest countries receiving 'special and differential treatment' which exempts them from many of the obligations. China acceded to the WTO in 2001, and Russian accession was finalized in 2012, making Iran the largest economy that is not a member.

In or out? The membership challenge

Many of the decisions made by the UN, the Bretton Woods institutions, and the WTO, have global ramifications that affect members and non-members alike. To the extent that these institutions can be thought of as legitimate sources of these decisions, this mainly stems from the fact that they are inclusive. At the heart of each of them lies a deliberative forum that includes all members — the General Assembly in the UN, the Board of Governors in the IMF and World Bank, and the WTO biannual ministerial assembly. The weighting given to individual voices in these forums is different: the UN and WTO are built on a one member, one vote system, while the Bretton Woods institutions have adjusted voting weights depending on a number of variables. Both have some intuitive appeal, and neither fully excludes any country from the decision-making process, but it is no accident that the former scores high marks for legitimacy and the weighted system higher marks for efficacy.

Effectiveness depends on the ability to act quickly and decisively. Both the UN and the Bretton Woods institutions implicitly recognize that negotiation between close to 200 countries is likely to be too cumbersome to produce decisive action. Where decisive and rapid decision making is required, even the UN delegates this to smaller bodies, such as the Security Council. Legitimacy is maintained by creating accountability to the more inclusive bodies—an attempt to parallel the relationship between the electorate and their representatives in a democratic state. Real power rests with a small number of individuals, but their actions are kept in line indirectly.

In the event of abuse, the wider bodies can act to restrict their actions, or restructure their institutions.

This system works if the supposedly representative bodies are able to come to decisions and these are regarded as legitimate. However, the chain of legitimacy is relatively weak. Ultimate control may lie with the General Assembly and the Board of Governors, but rarely do they exercise this control. Achieving substantive reforms in the institutions requires 'supermajorities': two-thirds in the UN and 85 per cent in the Bretton Woods institutions. For the most part, the powers of these governing bodies are delegated, and they practise little in the way of surveillance. As mentioned above, the voting shares and influence of different countries is heavily imbalanced. The management in the Bretton Woods system is relatively powerful—the Board rarely rejects proposals put forward by the management. Weak legitimacy restricts the ability of the institutions to effect changes in their member states—they have no legitimate claim to violate the right to sovereignty.

There are many positive things that could be said about the effectiveness of the global institutions in the post-war era. Whether they can deal with the emergent global challenges is a more open question. The problem lies in the method employed for balancing the competing demands of effectiveness and legitimacy.

Shifting Mandates

Historically the weakness of legitimacy was less problematic than you might expect. The Bretton Woods institutions did not start pushing for large structural reforms until the 1970s—in the post-war years ensuring economic stability was conceived of as a reactive rather than proactive role, and the main problem facing developing countries was generally thought to be under-capitalization. The IMF may have been run by a handful of industrialized countries, but these countries were also its main clients. Both of these bodies also enjoyed a reputation for competence—their work was technical and they were staffed by individuals who were seen to be amongst the most professional and to have unparalleled economic expertise. The IMF was available when it was needed, to fire fight when a country faced an economic crisis, and the World Bank had the necessary capital and expertise to provide loans for infrastructure that would enable growth. Initially, neither of these institutions was in the business of telling countries how to run their economies.

With the first oil crisis of 1973, the perceived role of these institutions changed. The emphasis within economics shifted to the importance of institutions, both for economic stability and for development. Wider conditionality was attached to the IMF and World Bank loans, demanding structural adjustment as a precondition for the receipt of funds. It was following this shift, from a primarily passive or reactive role to a more proactive direct involvement in economic management, that the Bretton Woods institutions became the subject of intense controversy.

It should be noted that the conditionality approach does not seem to violate sovereignty, provided the loan is accepted voluntarily. However, countries in the position of taking IMF and World Bank loans increasingly were in a straightjacket of economic crisis. The power of the Bretton Woods institutions increased as that of their clients eroded. In the 1970s, the cost of declining an IMF loan became economic collapse. World Bank loans are repaid over a much longer period and tend to be much cheaper than funding from other sources, if indeed funding at the scale and duration of World Bank funding is available from other sources, which typically for the countries most in need it is not. The more in need countries are, the more accurate is the widespread perception that the IMF and World Bank impose unwanted economic policies, since borrowing nations in crisis typically have no other option. The shift to proactive policies through which these institutions have become more powerful has eroded the claim to legitimacy.

The trade-off between legitimacy and effectiveness has also been played out in the UN, but with different outcomes. The structure of the Security Council was designed with an eye towards preventing destructive acts rather than promoting cooperation. The veto system means that proposals are easily blocked. Even if no veto is brought to bear on a system, the passage of a resolution still requires a weighty majority. As a result, it is very difficult for a country to receive UN support for an offensive operation. This creates some semblance of legitimacy, since resolutions that blatantly favour the interests of one group of countries over another are rarely enacted. It can be seen as a reaction to the weak chain of legitimacy, strengthening their limited mandate to interfere with the governance of their member states.

However, this structure is not suited to dealing with problems that are fast moving or controversial. The veto means that it is too easy for individual states to block the process.

In parallel to the Bretton Woods institutions, the UN's focus on legitimacy seems to be more suited to conservatism than activism. This may have been sufficient for the limited purposes for which it was created, but has resulted in disappointment for those hoping for effective global governance to meet evolving demands. Given the limitations of these institutions, is it reasonable to expect them to be able to deal with the emerging challenges outlined in Chapter 1?

Fiddling While Problems Escalate

The IMF already has some responsibility for global financial stability, shared with the Bank of International Settlements and the Financial

Stability Forum. The clear failure of these institutions to protect against the financial crisis should serve as a warning that the traditional multilaterals have little capacity to deal with financial risks. The failure of the IMF to prevent the economic crisis, despite its explicit mandate to prevent global economic instability, reflects a series of failures. Among these is the dominance of the governments represented on its Board over the staff. Indeed, the then Chief Economist, Raghuram Rajan, gave a prescient presentation in 2005 entitled 'Has Financial Development Made the World Riskier?' It identified much of what was to come.

Why, then, did the IMF not take action? First, far from Rajan reflecting an institutional view, he was challenging it, and his views were rejected by both the majority of his complacent colleagues and the US and other major G7 shareholders who saw only a downside in pricking the populist bubble of cheap credit. For the reasons provided above, the IMF lacks the power to demand substantive reforms from its members unless they are requesting a loan. Even if the IMF board had embraced the warnings of Rajan, which it did not, it is unlikely that it could have forced change on the world's major financial centres: New York and London. Indeed, anecdotal evidence suggests that the US Treasury Secretary was not engaged with the IMF regarding their concerns on the US economy, whereas an equivalent signal sent in a developing country would have required a personal response from the Finance Minister.[48]

The IMF could have issued recommendations or created pressure for reform. However, the governors of the IMF did not see the need. Public policy throughout much of Europe and in the US had supported the housing bubble, and continued to support the extension of homeownership to low-income families. Reforms to limit financial risk would have burst the economic bubble these countries were enjoying. Solutions that inflict short-term pain would have been unpopular everywhere but especially so in the US, where unemployment had only recently begun to recover from the dot-com bust.[49]

Given the power of the UK and US within the IMF, it is not surprising that the IMF did not attempt to fervently push for financial regulation. And we shouldn't be surprised that what warnings there were fell on deaf ears. In the final analysis, the power of the global institutions is circumscribed by its members. The more powerful members are most able to ignore the rules. In football, if the referee shows a red card, all players are compelled to respect the ruling. In global governance, even the most powerful institution, the IMF, would be unable to give effect to its rulings if the most powerful countries, such as the US or China, chose to ignore its verdict. By contrast, governments in desperate need of a financial lifeline have little option but to abide by the IMF's demands, as was the case for emerging markets during the debt crises of the 1970s, 1980s, and 1990s, and is the case today for Greece and other European countries suffering acute debt crises.

In fact, although Rajan was proved correct, his analysis was far from the consensus view. The complexity of the financial system meant that the growth in systemic risk was obscured. In addition, the ideological views of a pro-market group of economists, the Chicago or so-called freshwater school, had come to dominate thinking in the IMF. Within this framework, actors are conceived of as supremely rational, and markets are thought to price assets perfectly. For a proponent of the Chicago school, there is no such thing as a bubble. There is only an increase in prices driven by changing economic fundamentals. During the pre-crisis years, many were aware that rising house prices were the result of innovations in the financial markets. But these innovations were seen as fundamentally positive. Their destructive capabilities were not well understood. If we had possessed a more thorough understanding of the financial system, and the dominant institutions had been less captured by a narrow approach to economics, the pressure to reform finance would have been much greater.

Why did the IMF so readily adopt an extreme ideological framework? In part, it was simply reflecting the intellectual climate of the time. But it cannot escape blame completely. Its employees are drawn from a relatively homogenous group. They are almost all economists, and are almost all trained at one of a small group of American and British universities. This hiring practice leaves the institution open to intellectual and ideological capture. An added disability is that although the Bretton Woods institutions are the elite of the international civil service, they are far removed from the market, and led by long-serving professionals rather than market traders and practitioners. The institutions are distant from and unable to stay abreast of the evolving technologies that shape international finance and generate complexity and risk.

These factors all point to the limitations of the IMF as a leading force in the drive for financial stability. It lacks the strength and independence of a domestic regulator, and it lacks the legitimacy of a global legislature or the knowledge of a market participant. What power it has is exercised through ultimatum and persuasion, and these techniques are ineffective against countries which may choose to ignore its advice, such as the US. The IMF can do little to correct perverse incentives, but it could build capabilities and through diversity in recruitment and governance reform could become less prone to capture by intellectual fashions.

Governing Climate

There is no one institution with responsibility for the governance of the natural environment. A number of countries, particularly developing ones, have long called for the establishment of a 'world environmental organization' (WEO) to anchor global efforts for the environment, just as the WHO does for health and the WTO for trade. Leaders such as the Malaysian Prime Minister Mohd Najib bin Tun Haji Abdul Razak have called for a WEO which is consultative and helps to facilitate the participation of developing countries in environmental debates in a more meaningful way. This highlights an important sensitivity. Many developing countries feel that the dominant global organizations were designed and developed by the developed world, with the poorer countries on the sidelines. In climate talks, this sensitivity is particularly pertinent given that the burden of cutting carbon emissions may be passed to the largest developing countries, despite the fact that the urgent need to cut emissions arises out of decades or even centuries of emissions and environmental damage in the developed world.

It is not just developing countries that are calling for an overhaul of environmental governance. In 2009, in the lead-up to the infamous Copenhagen climate talks, Chancellor Merkel of Germany and President Sarkozy of France were also strong champions of an organization within the UN system with real political clout. This debate, and the climate debate more broadly, has now been overshadowed by economic uncertainty and crisis management. The idea of creating a WEO is likely to remain on the fringe.

As in many global institutions described previously, there are a number of international organizations with some mandate related to aspects of the environment and sustainable development. None have the institutional authority, funding, or legitimacy to deliver at the scale needed for today's challenges. The UN Environmental Programme (UNEP) is the most established. It was set up in 1972 with a mandate to be the leading global environmental authority. Yet its capacity to reach such an ambitious mandate is severely limited by resources. It has one of the lowest annual budgets in the UN system, apparently less than the price of a new Boeing 737.[50]

Beyond formal institutions, there is a bewildering array of agreements, multilaterals, panels, treaties, and targets related to global environmental issues. The track record suggests that existing multilaterals can do little to stop climate change. Despite the negative effects of carbon emissions being acknowledged by the UN-based International Panel on Climate Change (IPCC) as early as 1990, little substantive action has been taken. Simply importing high-emission products from countries where higher emissions are permissible, in order to reduce emissions at home, has become a favourite trick for those wishing to meet emissions targets. Consumers, through an understanding that what matters is the entire carbon life-cycle of the products they use, should not care whether goods are manufactured locally or abroad, as the impact on the atmosphere is the same wherever they are produced.[51]

The relevant multilaterals have been too weak to overcome the incentive problems that plague emissions reductions. For example, the Kyoto Protocol may be legally binding, but there is no enforcement mechanism, and incentives for the 191 signatories to comply are primarily voluntary. Ironically, it is the lack of a tough enforcement mechanism that has allowed the Kyoto Protocol to receive such widespread support. Any treaty that genuinely tied the hands of government would be unlikely to collect so many signatures. Even in the absence of an enforcement mechanism, and in the face of widespread failure to meet the targets, the US refuses to sign up and in 2011 Canada withdrew from the Protocol.

'Soft' power (persuasion, norm-setting, and so on) has failed to act as an effective substitute. Since there are no negative consequences to ignoring the treaty, Kyoto has had only a weak effect on the incentive structure facing governments. And since the incentive structure is the main obstacle to dealing with climate change, the treaty mechanism, at least in the Kyoto form, is inadequate to meet the scale of the challenge. The failure in 2012 of Rio+20 (the United Nations Conference on Sustainable Development) is yet another dismal reminder of the impotency at great cost in terms of budgets and lost opportunity of global summitry.

Cybersecurity Centre?

The global response to cybersecurity has also been paltry, both in terms of cybercrime and cyberaggression. Again, there is no central agency focused on this critical issue. No central organization or committed constituency of critical states is pushing for an accord, and the international calls from business and professional networks for this to be addressed are not sufficiently organized or coherent to have an impact.

The only notable international treaty is the Council of Europe Convention on Cybercrime. This treaty has sought to harmonize law internationally and to enable cooperation, rendering it easier to extradite and prosecute offenders. It was hoped that this would discourage criminal use of computers, both for monetary gain and as a vector for malicious attacks.

The Convention has met with limited success. The biggest problem is limited coverage: only thirty-one states have acceded to the Convention. Russia and China are both notable omissions. The former is a leading centre for organized cybercrime, whereas the latter hosts more Internet users than any other country. No countries in South America, Asia, or Africa have ratified it.

There is another problem with the international treaty approach. Negotiations on the Council of Europe Convention began in 1997. Even among the earliest of adopters, it didn't come into force until 2004. This is simply too slow a response to such a fast-moving problem.

There have been a number of other responses to promoting cybersecurity. NATO has recently become more involved in the prevention of cyberaggression, establishing a cyber defence centre in Estonia and promising to assist allies who find themselves under attack. The International Telecommunications Union (ITU), a specialized UN agency, has also become more active in this field. They have designed a toolkit to serve as a model for cybercrime legislation and created an early warning organization, the International Multilateral Partnership against Cyber Threats (IMPACT).

These piecemeal responses are effective on their own terms, but do not engage with the central problem of cybercrime—preserving the innovative capacities of the Internet while ensuring that users are reasonably secure. Building defences against attack, as NATO is attempting, may ensure that some enjoy a more robust Internet infrastructure. But it will not significantly deter attackers who target private, rather than public, infrastructure. It will also do little to limit the spread of malicious code.

These complex cybersecurity issues transcend national boundaries and leave all countries vulnerable. Whether a new agency is the answer or strengthened responsibilities of an existing one, we urgently need a unified front in international policy and associated governance to monitor the growing evidence of cybervulnerability, deter cyber risks, and offer response support where attacks are successful. But to be truly successful, such an agency must also have the mandate to enforce appropriate global regulations and the capacity to penalize countries that fail to comply. The benefits of such an ambitious governance regime remains worth pursuing.

Your Global Doctor: The WHO

The WHO and international health system have been remarkably successful in the prevention of pandemics. The WHO has been relatively effective as a capacity-building agency, spreading information about outbreaks and promoting best practice. Over 190 countries are signed up to the International Health Regulations (IHR), which require the development of minimum core health capacities and entail an obligation to notify the WHO of emergent public health problems.

The main problem arises when the demands of the WHO and IHR clash with the interests of states, as with the SARS epidemic. In these cases, the use of 'soft' power does seem to have enjoyed limited success. Following the failure of China to share information on a timely basis, a public admonishment by the WHO was issued. This was an unprecedented move, and seems to have provided sufficient incentives to prevent similar action by other states. China was fully cooperative during the H1N1 outbreak. In general, the level of compliance is high.

This is not to say that the WHO has always met with such success. International solutions tend to work through domestic solutions, and there can be strong opposition to internationally imposed standards. A key example is the HIV/AIDS pandemic. The promotion of an effective response to the pathogen has been hindered by political opposition, and the pressure exerted by the WHO on, for instance, South Africa's then President Thabo Mbeki met with limited success. Fortunately, the denial of treatment for AIDS is no longer supported by the South African government.

In 2007, Indonesia caused international uproar by refusing to submit samples of the H1N1 virus to the WHO. Such samples are critical to vaccine development, typically carried out within commercial labs. While Indonesia suffered the largest number of fatalities from the deadly virus, national officials were frustrated that viruses from their country could be used commercially to make a vaccine that they would not be able to afford.[52] They do raise a valid issue. Poor developing nations are often priced out of such critical medicines, and this is a serious problem that needs to be addressed. These actions severely undermine efforts to combat dangerous pandemics. The case highlights how easily domestic political opposition and commercial incentives can endanger global health security.

A larger problem is international inequalities in health care provision. Many developing countries still suffer from low capacity for disease response, due to poor quality infrastructure and a lack of trained professionals. This is worrying in itself, since it inhibits the ability of the country to respond to domestic health problems. But in the context of contagion effects, population growth, and urbanization, it may also result in an uncontrollable pandemic.

Surveillance and information sharing are at the heart of international health security. With an increasing share of the global population living in countries with poor capacity to respond to health threats, pandemics will once more become a significant problem. It is hard to see what the WHO can do to prevent this, regardless of how well it manages to coordinate information sharing and regulation. The WHO does sponsor a number of programmes that seek to improve access to medication and vaccines in developing countries, but it lacks the funding to make a significant impact on basic global health infrastructure. A step change in monitoring and surveillance to secure global coverage, together with a global capacity for rapid intervention to isolate potential pandemics at source, is urgently required.

Regional Players

There is no doubt that the global system is overwhelmed. What of the role of regional agencies, global sub-groupings, interest-based alliances, and other activities in these debates? Can some global issues be dealt with more effectively at a regional level?

Regional and sub-regional groupings potentially can play an intermediary role, connecting with nation states and providing shared capacity to exercise certain functions of global governance. Governance agreements do not operate in a vacuum, but interact with other agreements in complex ways.[53]

There are numerous high-profile regional bodies that serve as a platform for discussions on myriad issues, including trade, the environment, human rights, migration, and cybersecurity. Their purpose ranges from the political to the functional and technical. Each is distinct in terms of scope, 'power', and identity owing to the diversity of the countries participating and the issues covered.[54] While groups tend to form around issues, geography, or for specific purposes, the determination of which countries come together in the regional groupings is typically political.

The European Union

The EU has advanced rapidly to become the largest and most comprehensive regional body. Created in the aftermath of the Second World War, the EU has grown into a unique economic and political partnership among twenty-seven European countries. While under significant pressure in current times, the EU has successfully launched a single-market currency and progressively built a single Europe-wide market, enabling the free movement of people, goods, and capital among member states. Beyond economic partnership, the EU is now advancing the software (or institutions) of integration and the establishment of common standards and values, such as human rights and democracy, as well as the hardware, through its major investments in infrastructure and development.

Unlike the UN Charter, the European Court of Justice is able to legally enforce EU treaties among member states and can impose fines or sanctions for non-compliance. On the environmental front, the EU has established ambitious emission reduction targets and has created laws ranging from climate change concerns to noise pollution. Like many global institutions, the EU lacks the authority to enforce compliance. The failure of governments to abide by the key Maastricht economic criteria lies behind the crisis in the Euro, with major countries, including France, Germany, and much of Southern Europe, breaching the agreed rules.

The EU has moved beyond economic decision making to bring about a deeper integration of political agenda and social/cultural identity of its members. This attempt at harmonization differs from the cultural protectionism seen elsewhere, such as the North American Free Trade Agreement (NAFTA) between the US, Canada, and Mexico.[55] Its functional interdependence aims to promote a common identity and community among its members, while still protecting national identities and cultures. These have not been diluted despite closer integration.[56]

The Euro crisis illustrates the extent to which systemic risk has the potential to leap over national and industry boundaries, posing unanticipated and long-lasting cascading challenges. At the time of writing, the stability of the Eurozone remains gravely threatened. The existing institutions and mechanisms for political coordination appear unable to rise above national and short-term pressures to resolve the crisis.

The EU has been held up as the strongest example of a group of countries that willingly have given up key areas of national sovereignty in the interests of a collective European vision and shared framework for regional governance. Massive investment in regional institutions has been designed to underpin European integration. In finance, the European Central Bank and related mechanisms for managing the Euro and financial integration are among the most sophisticated of governance institutions anywhere. Their failure to overcome the governance challenges in Europe reinforces our concerns regarding the widening governance gaps which threaten to undermine progress in the 21st century.

G8 to G20 and beyond

For decades the emerging markets and a growing army of NGOs and commentators have been pressing for the replacement of the moribund G8 with a grouping that represents a far wider range of countries. The G20 (Group of Twenty Finance Ministers and Central Bank Governors) collectively accounts for more than 80 per cent of the global gross national product and of world trade, and had been meeting on the sidelines of the World Bank/IMF annual meetings for years. The financial crisis propelled this group into the limelight when, at the London Summit of 2009, the heads of state of the G20 countries met to discuss measures to resolve the crisis and agree on other matters. Optimism that this would prove a watershed in global governance has subsequently dissipated as the G20 has proved that, while it is more legitimate, it is as incapable as the G8 in terms of its ability to agree and effectively implement global agreements. It is a self-appointed group, with no executive power or capability, and as the secretariat is undertaken by the rotating Chair there is no continuity. Within a decade of its formation, the G20 has descended into yet another debating forum, unable to exercise effective global leadership.[57]

Other groupings include the Asia-Pacific Economic Cooperation (APEC), set up by Australia in 1983 in response to the perceived need for an arena for the Asia-Pacific region to engage and collaborate. It has a broad membership—with the US, Peru, Chile, and Russia part of this grouping. The Association of Southeast Asian Nations (ASEAN) has a more exclusive Asian identity and provides a voice to smaller, more economically vulnerable Asian states that may be overshadowed by China and India in regional debates.

Beyond Asia, there are similar organizations across the globe, such as the West African, Eastern, and Southern African communities and the Nafta, Mercosur, and Andean groups in North and Latin America. These regional and sub-regional groupings have enjoyed some success in addressing trade, commercial, and other regional concerns. However, they have no mandate or capability when it comes to addressing global issues. As a stepping stone to a global agreement, or when it comes to implementing global agreements, they potentially could play a valuable role.

Stepping Stones or Obstacles to Global Agreements?

Certain issues and agreements, such as trade, can be seen as moving from the regional agenda to fostering global consensus or best practice approaches. Jagdish Bhagwati has discussed whether regionalism will accelerate or inhibit multilateral trade liberalization.[58] Regional economic arrangements may boost multilateral openness through incentives for expansion and improving efficiency through simply reducing the number of members involved in negotiations.[59] For some other issues, such as agricultural trade reform, going from a regional-based agreement to a global one may well prove an effective stepping stone.

However, such a strategy may prove to be a major impediment to a global solution. The EU's common agricultural policy, through subsidies and protectionism, has grossly distorted world markets and made food in Europe cost much more than it should.[60] Protectionist policies have turned the EU from a food importer into the world's second largest exporter of foodstuffs, to the disadvantage of many developing-country exporters. European agricultural policy is now among the most significant stumbling blocks to the development round of trade negotiations. Subjecting the EU to global disciplines is essential to a global solution. The biggest and most powerful players, such as the EU, US, and Japan, are able to distort markets and create an uneven playing field which small and poorer players, notably developing countries, cannot compete on.

Regional groups are a distinct part of international governance, which on some issues, such as security, human rights, and trade agreements, have distinct advantages over nation states. Their role on the global stage is vital, they have legitimacy through their member states to act, and some have the bureaucratic capacity to manage some of the truly international concerns.

Are regional groups an aid or an obstacle to global governance? Do regional groups, like states, act for self-protection, making decisions on international problems in so far as they affect their own region rather than considering the global system as a whole? Those regional groups with greater bureaucratic structure and economic stability are in a position to obstruct decisions made by global institutions, blocking trade agreements or refusing environmental protocols, thus undermining global decision-making authority and preventing the resolution of global issues. These groups have the power and technical capacity to shift the terms of global debates and to greatly assist in the construction of global agreements.

However, they also have the power to frustrate such agreements, either through lack of political will or because they may simply lack the capacity and the jurisdiction to operate outside of their own region. Existing tensions between neighbouring countries, such as India and Pakistan, can also undermine the effectiveness of regional alignments.

Regional groups do not exist in isolation. Even relatively self-sufficient groupings face the consequences of global issues, as seen in the contagion of economic crises of the late 1990s. These issues can cascade rapidly across regions, as is evident in the crisis that has brought the EU to its knees. While regional institutions and agreements are a vital aspect of implementation and decision making in global governance, they have uneven capacity to act and are diverse in their interests and goals. For certain problems, such as pandemics and climate change, a regional response is not sufficient. They are not a substitute for a more overarching framework of global governance, given the lack of their incentives or capacity to act on a truly global level.

The Continuing Role of the Nation State

The death knell of the nation state has been sounded prematurely. While it was the inefficacy of the international system that took subprime lending from a domestic US issue to international catastrophe, it is to nation states that we look in order to clear up the mess and provide resolution. On the one hand, the nation state is seen increasingly as helpless or ineffective against the tide of international problems. Yet, on the other, it falls to domestic governments to take practical steps to deal with the fallout and, as seen with the widespread application of austerity measures in Europe, to bear the costs of mistakes and systemic inadequacies.

I have highlighted the issue of incentives. National politicians and electorates understandably have a national and often myopic view of international problems. It is this issue of perspective which is key to addressing the lack of willingness in tackling, and taking responsibility for, global challenges. National identities continue to trump regional and international concerns. Resolving this would go a considerable distance to addressing the concerns of this book. Economic, environmental, or other crises are blamed on the current leaders and government of the day, rather than being viewed as truly international systemic issues. This is perpetuated within domestic political debates, leading to reluctance to suffer the costs of bailing out regional neighbours. International agendas are set by participant nation states.

Despite this reticence by the citizenry, nation states remain the central actors in taking practical action on international concerns. Nations remain the strongest power-bases and bureaucracies in the international system. Maintaining sovereignty within their own borders has become harder, but this does not diminish the power of nation states on the global stage. It is clear that alone they are not capable of addressing the global concerns described in this volume. Yet it is worth remembering that it will fall to nation states to implement many of the decisions made by any new global governance institutions or arrangements.

Creativity Needed

The track record of the existing multilateral institutions on the challenges we are concerned with is patchy at best. We have shown that the global challenges are mounting, with increased connectivity, population growth, income growth, and urbanization all pointing to more rather than fewer complications. Even where the system functions well, as within the WHO, the capacity of the global institutions to deal with the coming workload is limited. We therefore need to consider whether these systems can be reformed at the scale and pace required, or whether more creative solutions will be necessary.

CHAPTER THREE

Rethinking Reform: Nations, Networks, and Knowledge

Where to from here? As outlined in Chapter 2, existing global governance structures are no longer fit for purpose and are ill-equipped to address the new and rapidly evolving challenges of the 21st century. Given the poor track record regarding the creation of new institutions, it is worth considering whether institutions such as the UN, World Bank, and the IMF could be radically reformed and re-energized for today's needs.

There have been decades of debates and discussions on ways to reform these lumbering global institutions, both within the organizations themselves and from external committees, governments, NGOs, and think-tanks. Numerous books and reports have been written on the topic, and this book does not intend to join this long procession and add to the paralysis of analysis on how best to reform existing global governance institutions.

However, it is important to recognize that a number of reforms of institutions such as the World Bank and the UN have been successful, and it is worth reflecting on what lessons can be drawn from these successes. This chapter will outline some fundamental changes that need to be injected into existing structures if they are to remain relevant in meeting new global challenges.

Despite reform efforts, existing institutions are unlikely to transform at the pace and scale required. Therefore, in this chapter I also explore the possibility that new and creative interventions could play a part in addressing global challenges.

Reform Rewards

The UN system has seen repeated reform efforts. Numerous committees and memoranda seek to encourage better alignment between the different agencies. Following the UN's Millennium Summit, the establishment of the Millennium Development Goals at its Monterrey meeting provided a laudable example of a common agenda around which international agencies, governments, and civil society have rallied. Establishing common goalposts, and through a succession of conferences in Rome, Paris, Accra, and Busan, a common set of rules, in coordination with the Development Assistance Committee of the OECD, has meant that for the first time the wide range of different actors can at least aspire to play on the same team. These reforms offer genuine progress within the development sphere.

The World Bank, IMF, and WTO have similarly evolved over time and are fundamentally different in terms of their activities and membership compared with when they (or the GATT in the case of the WTO) were established in the aftermath of the Second World War. However, the reform of global institutions has occurred at an evolutionary pace, with the UN, the Bretton Woods institutions, and others being forced to adapt due to pressures in a changing external environment, rather than taking a proactive approach to change. Too often reform discussions are focused on the minutiae of policy and bureaucratic processes, rather than the much needed bigger-picture perspective.

Another area of notable reform in the global governance system has been with respect to engaging business. The UN Global Compact was launched in 1999. It seeks to encourage businesses to adopt sustainable and socially responsible policies, and more ambitiously to acknowledge and enhance the role that corporations are playing in global governance. By 2012, 7,000 large firms from 150 countries had signed up to the Global Compact, with specific programmes in areas such as energy, climate change, women's empowerment, and anti-corruption.[61] The positive role played by business participants at the Rio+20 conference was highlighted as one of the few notable improvements in comparison with the original Rio Conference on Environment and Development in 1992.

However, the voluntary commitment of certain business leaders to self-policed standards is not a substitute for binding global agreements. Participation is purely voluntary and there is no scrutiny or action against non-compliance. While providing a forum and source of moral comfort, and even persuasion for global corporations, the limits of the Global Compact include its inability to ensure compliance even within its own small sample of members, let alone extending these laudable standards to the rest of the private sector.

To resolve global challenges we need to move beyond the evolutionary progress outlined above. For global governance institutions to become relevant, legitimate, and effective organizations for the 21st century, there are a number of fundamental characteristics that need to be embedded in their cultures and structures. These essential elements include those that are outlined in this chapter. They are not necessarily new ideas. A number have been on the agenda for some time, but their implementation has proved elusive.

The Non-negotiables

Without going into specific details for each organization, there are some headline reforms needed across most global governance institutions. If we can radically reshape existing structures with these high-level reforms, existing institutions will be more likely to become useful players in the fight against climate change, financial vulnerability, pandemics, cybersecurity, and beyond. Without such fundamental change in the critical areas examined here, they will remain unfit for 21st-century purpose and become increasingly moribund.

Genuine legitimacy

Legitimacy lies at the root of many of the criticisms facing global governance organizations. What gives these organizations the right to rule, where ruling includes developing rules and trying to secure compliance, either through incentives or penalties?[62]

The trade-off between legitimacy and the effectiveness of institutions has been discussed in Chapters 1 and 2. Legitimacy and legality are not necessarily the same, as the fierce struggle by the US and UK governments to secure UN consent to the invasion of Iraq attests. Securing an international system of governance that is legitimate and yet is not paralysed by veto is necessary. It also needs to be recognized that the consent of nations at the UN, or in other forums, to resolutions does not necessarily or even normally imply that the citizens of that nation agree with or are even aware of the resolution. In democratic countries with a robust media, a greater degree of awareness may be anticipated, but survey after survey in the US illustrates that the overwhelming majority of its citizens are unaware of key global issues.

Many have argued that the structures of global governance institutions, of 'chair and shares', are based on post-Second World

War formulas that are now obsolete. There are numerous proposals for different models of voting power and representational structures based on the economic or social weight of member countries. Not only do the foundations remain, but so does the entire edifice, so what emerges is an architect's nightmare of conversions, extensions, and divisions, with the officials being moved from one office to another, rather than building new structures that reflect changed circumstances and are designed to meet new challenges.

We need to find new ways to engender collective ownership and belonging. A shared global standard for legitimacy of global governance institutions is needed to bolster public support, strengthen institutional authority, and repair damaged perceptions. There is no doubt that the path to greater legitimacy within global governance structures is extremely difficult, as they struggle to connect to voters in the nations they supposedly represent. Citizens feel that they are too distant, non-accountable, and cannot be challenged directly. These criticisms will be difficult to overcome, but without a stronger connection to their constituency the ability of global institutions to have genuine impact is questionable.

Broader perspectives: increasing the skill base

The challenges of the 21st century require a new mix of skills and expertise that are different from those that these global institutions have traditionally attracted. Just as many national governments can struggle with 'career civil servants', global institutions also experience low staff turnover. This is in large part due to the highly competitive (typically tax-free) salaries, the institutional culture in which long service is the norm and often commensurate with promotion, as well as what might be described as 'comfortable' career paths.

Such organizational profiles are out of step with modern working trends. Senior personnel seldom have experience which extends outside the institution, and in the IMF, World Bank, and many UN agencies, it is common for the managers to have risen through the ranks over a thirty-year career, having entered in highly competitive 'young professional' cohorts immediately following their graduation. The lack of turnover and failure to integrate senior business and other professionals from outside the institutions mean that these organizations suffer from groupthink and a weakness in harnessing new ideas and innovation. The IMF and other institutions responsible for supervising the global financial system, for example, had not employed a critical mass of professionals with current trading and derivative skills among their many thousands of senior personnel. It is not surprising that they were taken by surprise and unable to fathom the implications of the explosion of derivative products.

A greater focus on attracting mid-career specialists, offering rotations, secondments, and recognizing equivalent skill sets achieved through alternative career paths and practical experience, would reinvigorate and broaden the organizational knowledge base. It is necessary to encourage new ideas and different approaches, and enable such organizations to build further capacity, particularly in skills and expertise more relevant to today's environment. For example, the IMF and financial regulators would benefit greatly from bringing successful architects of financial products into their organizations, although this would be difficult to manage, not least because of the conflicts of interest.

Building interdisciplinary teams is also important. The problems of the world do not define themselves in the scholarly stovepipes by which professionals are taught their academic skills. To address global challenges the perspectives of many disciplines are required, as is bridging across the different global challenges. So, for example, bringing in climate specialists to work with the WHO on the tracking of human pathogens and their links with avian migration patterns could enable a better ability to predict pandemics.[63] International organizations would also benefit immensely from collaboration with other institutions, governments, and those with specialist knowledge, perhaps recruited for the duration of specific projects to foster innovation and problem-solving. Recruiting locally on specific national projects is also vitally important—both to ensure relevant local knowledge is captured as well as for fostering a sense of local ownership for the initiative.

Coming into focus

The world has moved on since the mandates of the IMF, the World Bank, the UN, and other international agencies were defined some sixty years ago. The picture of global governance today is one of duplication, ambiguity, overlap, and confusion. Mandates have stretched and arguably lost the clarity and direction much celebrated upon their establishment. The UN reform task force on which I served identified a dozen agencies with overlapping responsibility for water.

No agency was prepared to give up its engagement, as each saw its role as special, with their particular biases reinforced by particular governments, charities, and lobby groups. In the case of development there is even greater overlap, with governments assigning numerous responsibilities that are also the preserve of the UNDP or other agencies to their own domestic aid agencies or the World Bank. The reasons for this relate in no small part to the view held by the US, EU, and Japan that they are more able to influence the Bretton Woods institutions, due to the voting and shareholder arrangements, and also that these institutions are more effective than the UN agencies, even if they lack comparable legitimacy.

The mounting evidence of numerous task forces on global governance reform points to the need for rationalization. A renewed effort should be made by governments and their representatives on the boards of the different agencies to force the heads of all major institutions to come together and consider where they fit into the bigger picture of the global framework. There is a need to clarify roles, remove duplication, and define mandates that enable them to better address contemporary global challenges. This may sound naïve and ambitious, but the wasted efforts and opportunity costs associated with global institutions working in their historical silos while orphan issues have no institutional home, require that the global governance system redoubles its efforts to rationalize and reform to meet new challenges.

The reform of mandates must also be continuous, with greater flexibility built in to enable these organizations to respond to new challenges, and also embrace unexpected opportunities. This requires fixed-term, rather than tenured, employment contracts. All work programmes should be for a fixed duration and rigorously evaluated by credible external parties, rather than being established without an exit strategy or automatically being extended and renewed. In order to ensure that individuals on fixed-term contracts work to achieve longer-term aims, it would be necessary to identify agreed landmarks along the road that may be seen as staging posts in the achievement of global and longer-term objectives.

Given the complexity and gravity of today's economic, security, social, and environmental challenges, global institutions need to appreciate their responsibility, not only to today's generation but to future generations. There is an alarming absence of long-range thinking within global structures, just as there is at the national and business levels. Whether on issues of economic reform, pandemic control, migration management, or climate change, the scale of the challenges means that countries and organizations with the capacity to think and plan over the longer term hold a strategic advantage. Whilst democratic governments are constrained by short-term electoral realities, many global institutions work on longer timeframes. The World Bank, for example, has great potential for fostering long-term thinking and investment, given that the average period of its loans is around twenty-five years, five times longer than the length of the electoral term of many national governments.[64]

Global leaders for global issues

The Director-General of the WTO, Pascal Lamy, has argued that the failure of leadership is one of the most pressing challenges facing global governance today.[65] Lamy can take pride in being an elected leader of a global institution, with his position having been contested by candidates from Mauritius, Brazil, and Uruguay.

This is not the norm. Closed-door agreements have usurped what ought to be a merit-based search for the best candidate. The US nominates, historically without opposition, the President of the World Bank. The Managing Director of the IMF is agreed by the European nations, and although there have been three cases where non-Europeans have been considered, since its inception only European candidates have been appointed. In 2012, despite widespread disenchantment with the process, and the unprecedented nomination of two alternative candidates for consideration by the Executive Directors, predictably the World Bank President Robert Zoellick was replaced by a US national. While there is little doubt that President Obama's nominee Jim Yong Kim is an able public-health specialist, he would probably not have emerged from a global competition as a front-runner for the Presidency of the World Bank.

The reliance on an antiquated deal, forged at the establishment of the Bretton Woods institutions in 1946, fundamentally undermines the institutions that are clearly seen to be unrepresentative of the world that they purport to work for and represent. Developing countries now account for over half of the global economy, a significant change from the 10 per cent or so at the formation of the Bretton Woods institutions. Developing countries represent six billion of the seven billion world population, yet it is still developed countries which hold majority voting shares and control the leadership of these institutions.[66] The case for a developing country candidate is not simply about representation, but finding a candidate with hands-on experience and proven leadership in meeting development challenges.

If we are to meet the challenges of the 21st century, we need to draw on the most capable professionals and managers, whatever their nationality. The rapid growth in education and management experience around the world, and especially in emerging markets, should be a source of enormous optimism as there has been an explosion in the capabilities needed to address global challenges. We urgently need to widen the pool of candidates for staff and leadership positions, and ensure that the full potential of the global pool of talent is recognized. This process would simultaneously achieve greater regional balance and more equity in representation across the global governance institutions, while achieving higher levels of effectiveness.

Getting the job done

Effectiveness needs to be our central concern. If they are not effective, there is no point in investing in global institutions. Effectiveness is about the capacity of global institutions to mobilize resources, to address problems of international dimensions, and to deliver tangible, visible results against transparent and measurable benchmarks that are determined in advance. It is difficult to respect organizational leadership or to claim legitimacy if the institution is not able to work efficiently. Legitimacy also feeds into effectiveness and makes it a more able partner.

As Pascal Lamy has argued, 'the main challenge is that the Westphalian order gives a premium to "naysayers" who can block decisions, thereby impeding results. The enduring viscosity of international decision making puts into question the efficiency of the international system.'[67]

Nation states often resist transferring or sharing their jurisdiction with international institutions, while at the same time they are often too busy dealing with domestic concerns to dedicate sufficient attention to issues requiring international agreement, such as those relating to climate or trade. Global summits have all too often become talking forums, unable to reach binding decisions and lacking the authority and willingness to commit to global targets and timeframes. Given the sheer scale of the potential threats on the horizon, such endeavours seem indulgent and of questionable value.

Reimagining the World: The Hunt For New, Creative Approaches

All of these reforms are extremely important and urgently needed. However, given that discussions on efficiency, legitimacy, and leadership have been conducted ad nauseam, I am not confident that we will see such revolutionary reforms of these institutions any time soon. It is important to continue to push for these reforms and maintain pressure on existing institutions to adapt to the needs of the 21st century. Given the scale and pace of the 21st-century challenges considered in this book, we also need to be thinking of creative alternatives through which to address them.

The solutions are unlikely to lie in establishing new global governance institutions. I fear they too would face similar legitimacy and jurisdictional difficulties, and be captured by vested interests. Equally, the solution is not to load more mandates onto existing institutions. We need to look for more imaginative solutions—beyond the usual suspects—and leverage the enormous potential that comes through globalization and today's hyper-connectivity.

Narrowing the world: a 'coalition of the willing'

Although the various challenges are formidable in different ways, they all share one feature: addressing them requires international cooperation. As seen in Chapter 2, the international status quo deploys several inadequate devices to address these challenges, from conditional bilateral aid to issue-specific summits and the UN Security Council. If we are to face this century's challenges we must find a mechanism for more effective international decision making and implementation. Navigating the 21st century requires that we forge a new means of cooperation.

What unites our present cooperative solutions is their respect for state sovereignty: all action taken through these channels is conceived as if it is authored by the states themselves. Yet this institutional framework is at times based on an outdated concept of sovereignty. The way we conceive of the state feeds into the way we achieve compromise, and therefore lies at the heart of our current inability to provide swift and responsive policies to emerging challenges. We do not need to reject state sovereignty, but we do need to revise our understanding of it, what it can achieve, and why it is valuable to us.

Fortunately, with the exception of pandemic eradication, and potentially world-destabilizing terrorist or nuclear activities, most global problems do not need unanimous action on the part of all states. If a critical majority of states can be persuaded to participate in regulation or more direct action, the recalcitrant minority may be tolerated. Accepting that they are unlikely to subscribe to global rules may be vital if any progress is to be made. For issues of global gravity, the 'coalition of the willing' may be persuaded that the domestic cost of inaction is greater than the potential benefits of a more comprehensive international distribution of the burdens of action. In the case of climate change, the refusal of the three nations responsible for almost half of all carbon emissions to cooperate must be overcome, even though most other states are willing to abide by global rules.

A 'coalition of the willing' has the advantage of effective hard power. This, however, does involve a trade-off against the legitimacy of a unanimous decision. The UN Security Council, for example, can grant a powerful stamp of legitimacy to that which it endorses because its resolutions are so vulnerable to permanent members' vetoes. The threats we face do not always afford us the privilege of such strong legitimacy. The Security Council is continually held up by the obstinacy of one or two members: for example, in January 2007 China and Russia, with South African support, vetoed a resolution urging Burma to release political prisoners and speed the transition to democracy, and more recently Russia and China have vetoed sanctions against Syria. In situations such as these the legitimizing benefits of full agreement are offset by the delegitimizing effect of a continual impasse.

The clearest impediment to effective global action is giving some states a veto. A reformed UN aiming to deal with contemporary challenges would have to replace this mechanism. One might start from a base requirement of a two-thirds majority. In deference to the vast inequalities in the capabilities of different states, and the realpolitik needed to allow powerful actors a degree of leverage if one is to retain their involvement in the process, it would be advisable to accord further influence to 'critical actors', that is, those states with the greatest capability in relation to a given specific issue.

Climate change governance

A preferable weighting system would vary from issue to issue, and indeed might vary depending on the aspect of the issue at hand. This is the idea of variable geometry. An issue can be broken down into a string of decisions. Climate change, for example, involves at least two steps: first an agreement on carbon emissions reduction targets; then an agreement on the transfer of technological expertise required to meet those targets. In each case, different groups of countries may be involved.

Any effective agreement on climate change requires the central involvement of two critical actors, the US and China. The US is by far the largest contributor to the stock of greenhouse gases due to its economic growth over the last century. China now accounts for the largest flow due to its extremely rapid industrial growth over the last thirty years. These countries, together with the other ten countries that account for over 90 per cent of global stocks and flows of greenhouse gases, are indispensable in the first discussion regarding arresting the rise in greenhouse gases.

So too are the countries that have the most to lose from climate change. Thus the discussion on curtailing and reducing emissions necessarily should include countries such as the Maldives and Bangladesh, which are at risk from rising sea levels (a one-metre rise is predicted to submerge the former and inundate 30 per cent of the latter).

In order to keep the number of participants to a manageable minimum, certain countries might be chosen to represent others in a similar predicament. The Maldives and Tuvalu (both island nations at risk from rising sea levels) could speak for each other, and Nepal and Bhutan (both nations facing floods and landslides from melting glaciers) might similarly send a joint representative. Similarly the countries of the Sahel where devastating famines are a growing peril could form a single constituency.

The challenge here is how to create constituencies among otherwise independent and even hostile states without prejudging the outcome of the debate. Many precedents exist for this, including at the World Bank and IMF where single constituencies at times represent the interests of up to twenty countries.

Once the emissions targets are agreed to, the focus turns to the 'how' of implementation. One vital aspect of this is the transfer of technologies to developing countries that allow them to reduce the carbon intensity of their development. Here, in contrast to the negotiation on overall targets on emissions, China would be across the table from the US.

The advantage of dividing an enormous and apparently intractable negotiating challenge, such as that of limiting climate change, into its separate components is one of concentrating the discussions and minimizing trade-offs between the different aspects of the issue. With one comprehensive negotiation, there is the constant risk that countries free ride on each other's detrimental actions rather than make a mutual commitment to solve their harmful practices. This risk cannot be eliminated, however: a country like China might still leverage its strong position in the first set of discussions to obtain favourable terms in the second aspect. If this trade-off is the only way to achieve clear agreement it may need to be tolerated. Concessions may need to be made to the powerful if their participation is to be guaranteed.

Accepting that not all global problems require global participation is crucial to solving them. The key is to get the critical parties—the countries (and/or corporations) that account for the problem, and those that represent the most affected—to come to agreement. If the result is a global agreement that only binds 90 per cent of the key players for many problems, it is far better than no binding agreement at all. Even where there is a real risk that those left out may free ride and even destabilize the global accord—such as is the case with failed states that become safe havens for terrorist groups—it may well be advantageous to get the rest of the world to agree a course of action, including actions which will bring the outsiders into the global tent.

At the heart of the problem of global governance is the need to persuade powerful states to act against their perceived self-interest. Some countries believe they would gain from climate change—rather than shirking the burdens of cooperation they actually believe they have a material interest in the negative global outcome. For example, there may be those in Russia, Canada, and other states in northern latitudes that believe they may benefit from warmer temperatures. They also believe that higher temperatures are likely to melt the Arctic ice and create new opportunities for oil and other resource extraction in their neighbouring waters, as well as opening the northern passages to shipping. However, these countries are gambling on only one aspect of climate change: that there will be average increases in temperatures. They are not taking account of uncertainties and the full range of possible outcomes, including, for example, the easing of the North Atlantic Gulf Stream, which could result in a precipitous plunge in northern European temperatures or wildly accentuated fluctuations in weather with potentially disastrous consequences for agriculture and human settlement.

In the face of a persistent minority of recalcitrant states, the gravity of global problems requires us to take further measures.

The only remaining option might be some form of sanction. This might operate directly through legislation, or indirectly through an internationally coordinated encouragement of issue-specific consumer choice. In the case of sanctions against apartheid South Africa, for example, the combination of consumer boycotts and sanctions by professional bodies, including various sporting authorities, served to reinforce the pressure on the regime and accelerate the end of apartheid. A critical majority of multinational corporations may be willing to make issue-sensitive choices themselves if there is enough momentum behind the issue, perhaps led by an international institution, such as is the case with the Equator investment principles championed by the International Finance Institution.

This is not always easy, as the West's relationship with oil-producing countries over the last half-century has demonstrated. Sanctions also require international coordination to be effective, especially if the states in question have the ability to retaliate with sanctions of their own, or simply ignore global opinion and be sustained by a small coterie of other like-minded rogue states. The inability of major powers to agree sufficiently binding or painful sanctions, as is the case with Iran and North Korea, also hampers effectiveness.

Shifting sovereignty

As we look for new solutions to today's challenges, we also need to shift our understanding of sovereignty to make it relevant for the 21st century. To borrow Isaiah Berlin's language from another context, our institutions need to shift from embodying sovereignty as 'sovereignty from' external coercion by foreign powers to embodying it as 'sovereignty to' the interests of one's citizens.[68] As the most serious of the threats facing a nation state—from the economic to the environmental—grow increasingly global in their roots and in their solutions, it no longer makes sense to see state sovereignty as grounded in its ability to prevent other agents from interfering with its territory. Rather, a state's power is better measured in its ability to harness the capacities of its global peers to solve those perils whose nature disregards national borders. As Bob Keohane and Joe Nye have argued for decades, globalization has shifted the locus of power from 'hard' military intimidation to 'soft' cultural attraction. Our view of sovereignty needs to catch up.[69]

We need to imagine a world where sovereignty is not just about preventing but also about enabling. If we redefine sovereignty, to look beyond coercion and exclusion but also consider cooperation and inclusion, it no longer makes sense as something one can monopolize. Anne-Marie Slaughter calls the former view of international relations, in which decision making is seen as concentrated at the very top of government, the view of the 'unitary state'.[70] She suggests that this view is growing progressively out of date, as international cooperation increasingly takes place between lower-level public-sector agents: judges, regulators, and legislators come together to find collaborative ways to solve common problems that each of them faces in a particular guise in their own countries.

Transnational networks

While the bulk of hard power is held by national governments, these transnational networks of public-sector professionals have limited discretionary authority at the domestic level. Combining this meagre hard power with that of their international counterparts, through the alchemy of soft power, may provide an incremental means to solve certain cross-border challenges, task by task. As Slaughter puts it, the 'unitary state' is in the process of 'disaggregation' and in certain dimensions is being replaced by networks that operate globally.[71]

The most prominent instances of these transgovernmental networks are the UN specialized agencies such as the Universal Postal Union, the International Civil Aviation Organization, and the International Meteorological Organization and global institutions such as Interpol. These agencies bring together like-minded professionals with converging interests, professional backgrounds, and common approaches to problem-solving. Transgovernmental networks are not a panacea, but if we are to provide a more effective response to global 21st-century challenges, they have considerable potential to address specific issues. As Slaughter puts it, 'networked threats require a networked response.'[72]

Transgovernmental networks that directly manage cross-border issues have several clear advantages over mediation by multilateral institutions. Whereas top-level government officials balance competing domestic interests and electoral concerns when devising their position in international negotiations, the various parties in transgovernmental networks are able to focus specifically on the common problem they face. Because they only represent a fragment of their state, they do not have to balance finding an effective solution against, say, competing interests that may have a strong influence over national governments.

If professional networks are tasked with solving the problem at hand, and each realizes that they can only achieve their domestic goals through a combined effort, there are fewer incentives to avoid cooperation. The police forces or environmental regulators of different nations, for example, are not in competition with each other, so even though their national governments might have sought to shift burdens onto each other, the regulators themselves would be more readily willing to share expertise and experience, and elaborate on common solutions to common problems.

This focused motivation to solve the problem at hand through cooperation is further reinforced by regular face-to-face relationships. Participation from the early stages of policy elaboration gives these agents a sense of ownership in the policy itself, and close interaction with peers imbues them with a personal stake in achieving outcomes they can be proud of. Professional pride among peers transcends national boundaries, and this can serve to reinforce the effectiveness of transgovernmental networks. In contrast to voluntary targets established by the UN or the Bretton Woods institutions, when these targets are established through consensus amongst professionals in transgovernmental networks, they tend to be pursued with a commitment which would be difficult to achieve if they were simply handed down from a government ministry. Nevertheless, the soft power of these networks can have significant results, for the judges, regulators, and other professionals who constitute these groups have considerable authority in their domestic institutions.

Transnational networks thus have the potential to accentuate our incentives for cooperation by trimming the group of participants down to those who have been charged with solving challenges at a domestic level. They can reach clear-headed assessments of the challenges ahead, and can make great headway in the harmonization of standards and in the sharing of information. In some cases, this constitutes significant progress in itself. The SARS outbreak, as we saw in Chapter 1, posed a serious threat in early 2003, not because the Chinese government had not detected it in its early stages, but because news of its spread was initially not shared. With an international professional ethic and practice of sharing pandemic information, the virtually costless act of giving other nations' health sectors early warning via the WHO would have been a matter of mere routine; concern for China's international reputation would have reinforced this rather than having discouraged it, as subsequent positive engagement by China has demonstrated.[73]

Furthermore, even more substantive acts on the part of networks need not necessarily meet opposition from governments. The fluid exchange of expertise and assistance through the WHO's Smallpox Eradication Programme played an indispensable part in overcoming lack of capability in certain developing countries, and thus in eradicating smallpox.[74]

Transgovernmental networks form a necessary and significant part of the response to global challenges that could be expanded to even greater effect. Yet such networks have limitations and their role should not be overstated. The relatively well-developed global network of finance professionals did not prevent the financial crisis.

Transnational networks are not immune to pressure from the governments to whom the individual agencies are answerable, and those networks and their governments are not always immune to lobbying from the private sector or narrow vested interests. As we saw in Chapter 2, a key challenge in coordinating our response to 21st-century threats is that capable states seek to minimize their own actions and do not simply pass the burdens of cooperation on to each other. This behaviour is most tempting to national governments when the costs of cooperation or the domestic benefits of the globally undesirable outcome are greatest, and in such circumstances it is unrealistic to expect individual agencies to act outside or have powers that exceed those enforced through national policy.

Sharing or competing incentives

The position of Indonesia with regard to what Indonesian Health Minister Siti Fadilah Supari called 'viral sovereignty', as we identified in Chapter 2, is relevant in this respect. Indonesia was the origin of 'the vast majority of repeated avian flu outbreaks' between 2004 and 2008.[75] Yet, since 2005, 'Indonesia...shared with the WHO samples from only two of the more than 135 people known to have been infected with H5N1 (110 of whom have died).'[76]

Furthermore, the Indonesian government stopped 'providing the WHO with timely notification of bird flu outbreaks or human cases'.[77] The reasoning behind this was that 'nations own any viruses that they discover within their boundaries, have the right to refuse sharing them with the WHO or any other foreign entity and may demand all profits derived from vaccines and other products made from those viruses'.[78]

Laurie Garrett suggests that the underlying fear of professionals in the Indonesian Health Ministry was that the WHO might not be able to manufacture more than 400 million vaccines. By turning virus samples into their property, they endowed themselves with a potent bargaining chip in possible negotiations for distribution of those vaccines.[79] The situation of scarcity introduces such high stakes that governments are prepared to jeopardize mutually beneficial cooperation in order to secure their primary interests.

Where the state's incentive to shift the burdens of cooperation onto other countries is great, regulators simply do not have the independence from central government to set ambitious emissions reduction targets backed up by robust enforcement regimes. Where there are powerful vested interests, such as in the financial or energy sectors, transnational networks do not facilitate a circumvention of entrenched disputes between sovereign states, but serve as an arena for their reappearance. Some problems simply cannot be addressed without the hard power of a willing executive, and in these cases public-sector professionals—legislators, judges, regulators—will not possess sufficient independence or authority to effect the change required.[80] With carbon emissions reduction or the financial sector, for example, the economic stakes are so high that the relevant regulatory and enforcement agencies cannot circumvent their national governments' attempts to shift the burdens of cooperation onto other nations.

An area where professional networks can make a significant difference is in helping to address the required missing pieces of information and responses to particular potential threats. Such activities may overcome the dangers inherent in states where expertise is lacking, for example with respect to viral threats and pandemics. It is relatively simple to see how incentives may be aligned in areas such as the threat of diseases that cross borders. The greater challenge is ensuring cooperation where incentives are not aligned.

Soft and hard power

The lack of substantial hard power makes for difficulties in any problems involving significant conflicts of interest. These might manifest themselves as an inability on the part of governments to confront powerful private-sector lobbies and tighten regulation, or simply unwillingness on the part of states to compromise with each other. With corporations holding so much power in the global economy, any proposed reform to our global institutions requires rising above the vested interests of both individual countries and the most powerful transnational companies. Yet pushing directly for the hard power of the law to require corporations to achieve desired outcomes is often on its own ineffectual.

To help transgovernmental networks to deal more effectively with global problems, the establishment of supportive groups that are able to transcend national interests is helpful. Keohane and Nye emphasize the importance of mitigating conflicts of interest that constrain countries, and the potential role of media and communication in shaping credibility in an age of information.[81] Slaughter highlights the extent to which activities associated with governments that are seen to be legitimate come to possess credibility.[82]

Even unilaterally commissioned research reports, such as the UK's Stern Review, achieve worldwide prominence in virtue of their authors' perceived legitimacy and their working within a framework established by an accountable state. Multilateral efforts such as the IPCC, which was created in 1989 by the UN Environmental Programme and the World Meteorological Organization, appear to many to be less credible than the initiatives of single states. This reflects the powerful attractiveness of notions of sovereignty and the continued importance of shared national identity. In fact, the IPCC, by bringing together leading scientists and expertise from over a hundred countries, should be both more credible and legitimate than the views of scientists, however eminent, from only one country.

Part of the challenge is one of communication. If the information is pitched at a level accessible to the general public—as is the case with the Stern Review, but less so with the IPCC—it can contribute to a groundswell of opinion that filters through to consumer choice or the ballot box. Yet credibility alone cannot achieve ambitious targets in halting climate change or achieving financial stability. The data and modelling analysis is highly complex and the distributional and other consequences subject to great uncertainty.

An added complication in finance is that the relevant information is shrouded in corporate secrecy. Similarly, in areas such as cyber and other security a combination of technological complexity and the fact that much of the information and interest in the issue is the domain of secretive national intelligence and other security agencies reduces the knowledge and trust of citizens who may regard these issues as beyond their expertise and involvement.

Networks of public-sector professionals have a powerful role to play in establishing rules-based global systems. But the boundaries of their competence and power, and their potential capture by national interests, needs to be recognized. The profit motive also undermines the potential for private-sector groups to collaborate in areas of emerging technology or, for example, in discussions which seek to weaken certain dimensions of the international intellectual property regime.

The experience of the WTO shows that once inside a rules-based body, even the powerful are forced by a combination of peer pressure and their own self-interest to abide by the rules. The WTO has brought immense benefits to the US, not least in bringing China, the EU, and other trade heavyweights under the same surveillance and sanctions regimes and by encouraging the incremental lowering of obstacles to trade.

The fact that trade is a political football within the US makes membership even more important, as it significantly reduces the extent to which the administration feels forced to succumb to the interests of any one lobby group or political populism and expediency. In providing a degree of insulation from short-term political pressures relating to daily decision making in trade, membership of the WTO removes a key uncertainty for domestic and foreign investors in the US and other economies that subject themselves to WTO rules. Rule-based systems increase international legitimacy and predictability. By preventing commercial and other bullying, they can also be an important source of protection for weaker countries, which are able to subject even the most powerful countries to the agreed standards.

Limits

By circumventing the most powerful agents in a sovereign state, networks forfeit some capability in terms of hard power, but also narrow the cooperating parties down to a level where there is a greater degree of shared interest, and thus potential to reach suitable compromises. The threat that 'weakest link' states pose to pandemic prevention can be countered with a free flow of information and assistance from regulators from stronger countries who have a clear self-interested stake in the weaker state reaching adequate capability. The weak state's regulators can learn from the mistakes of the stronger state's regulators, and by helping it the latter are fulfilling their own domestic objectives.

Global networks of public-sector professionals, working in tandem with expert and motivated NGOs to scrutinize voluntarily transparent corporate information, have a better chance of undermining conflicts of interest and mobilizing government hard power. In the face of the hardest threats, however, where the cost of action is high and interests are entrenched, global solutions require state-level coordination, and this requires both an effective decision making body, and the ability to threaten those nations who do seek to circumvent its resolutions with sanctions.

The business end of things

Beyond country collaborations and transnational networks, the private sector could also provide more leadership and active engagement in the management of global challenges. Business is just as vulnerable to climate change, financial crises, cyberattacks, migration mismanagement, and pandemics as governments and society at large.

Rising temperatures and sea levels, increased numbers of extreme weather events, and global warming have enormous implications for the agricultural sector, insurance, tourism, and transport industries, and many other businesses on different scales. The damage of the recent financial crisis has hit the bottom line of almost all businesses—from the biggest banks to small to medium-sized companies across the world. Business is often the target of cyberattacks, which bring significant financial but also reputational damage. In 2011, for example, the corporate giant Sony fell victim to cyberattack, with the perpetrators stealing the personal account details of over seventy-seven million PlayStation users and twenty-five million PC Games accounts.[83]

Business needs to be seen as a necessary part of the solution, capable of dedicating significant financial and intellectual resources to the issues as well as contributing to the development of innovative new approaches or technologies to confront the challenges. While much is made of the potential profits to be gained from new technologies which would assist in addressing global problems—from solar panels and electric vehicles to new vaccines and private security systems—the more important contribution of business is in being a responsible part of society with a vested interest in durable global solutions.

The World Economic Forum, World Business Council for Sustainable Development, UN Global Compact, and numerous other organizations, are seeking to engage business more effectively in local, national, and global problem-solving. In addition to norm-setting and informing their members as to what is considered to be global best practice, these bodies serve to bring leadership from the private and public sectors together with a view to establishing a platform for engagement and alignment around common goals.

Global businesses manage to overcome many of the challenges that bedevil international management in the public sector. Companies such as Apple or Toyota could no doubt have lessons for the public sector about operating across cultures and politics in real time while addressing constantly shifting technologies and political and consumer sentiment. In parallel to the growing gap between the global problems and institutions is the growing divide between the revolutions in management of global private-sector enterprises with international operations and their public-sector counterparts who remain trapped in a bygone era of management. This divide needs to be closed so that the public sector and global governance can benefit from the advances in management which are commonplace in the operation of global businesses.

New roads to innovation and transparency

There may also be untapped potential for the private sector to become directly involved in assuming some of the responsibilities of global problem solving. Any involvement of the private sector in these issues will be naturally subject to questions of conflicts of interest, or prioritizing corporate gain at the expense of vulnerable local populations or the natural environment. Corporate innovation and research and development are often guarded heavily, and the sharing of methods and innovation at times is heavily circumscribed by patents and fears regarding undermining corporate competitiveness. This could limit opportunities for more open innovation through cooperation and collaboration with governments, industries, universities, and research institutes.

Within the constraints of competitive business environments, new ways need to be found to leverage the expertise and resources of the private sector to address global challenges, not least through supporting new approaches. We need to find ways to foster partnerships with industry, NGOs, and the academic community. Similarly, more openness and transparency by the corporate sector will assist in building trust, particularly within highly sensitive communities and industries in poorer countries.

It is important not to be naïve about the interests of business. Indeed, in a number of cases, private sector interests may be directly opposed to a global solution. The lobbying power of US coal interests has been shown to be behind the erosion of public support for actions on climate change, just as that of the financial services industry was behind the drive for deregulation and resistance to constraints on their behaviour. Similarly, in agriculture the lobbying power in the US and Europe of major producers of grains, sugar, and cotton is behind the economically disastrous and highly regressive protectionist policies.

The effectiveness of these lobby groups is testimony of the power of organized groups to effect and resist change. While less than 0.1 per cent of the US or European population benefit from agricultural protection, and citizens in the EU and US on average pay over 1,000 euros or dollars per year more than they should for food, the perverse subsidies are testimony to the power of lobbies to capture national politics and subvert global agreement.[84]

In some cases, the private sector can be convinced to submit to transparency requirements in exchange for the reputational benefits of association with particular networks. NGOs may then be able to cooperate with the relevant public-sector professionals in pooling their domain-specific expertise and monitoring private-sector activities through this voluntarily provided information. Although set up by international NGOs rather than public-sector professionals, the umbrella organization 'Publish What You Pay' demonstrates what can be achieved. It encourages mining and oil companies to be transparent about the fees they pay to the governments of thirty resource-rich states, from Kazakhstan to Zambia, and encourages those governments to publish the fees they receive. Local NGOs in such states can then use this information to monitor how their governments are spending the money earned from the extraction of the country's natural resources.[85]

The Extractive Industries Transparency Initiative, launched at the World Summit for Sustainable Development in 2002, is a partnership between countries (such as the UK, US, and Netherlands, and developing countries such as Niger, Mauritania, and Timor-Leste) as well as participating companies (including ExxonMobil, Royal Dutch Shell, BP, and financial firms such as Standard Life), the World Bank, and NGOs. The NGOs play a pivotal role in involving civil society and holding the partners accountable to the agreement. Their role, in identifying transgressions and in pressurizing firms and countries to subscribe to the principles, has been significant. Another innovative approach is that developed by the Sudanese entrepreneur Mo Ibrahim, whose Foundation monitors governance in Africa and offers generous cash incentives to democratically elected African heads of state who deliver major steps forward in development and then voluntarily transfer power after their term expires. The index and prize seek to advance good governance through transparency, peer pressure, and cash incentives.

Voluntary agreements, such as Publish What You Pay or the Extractive Industries Transparency Initiative, work best in consumer industries, where the stamp of evaluation serves as a simple and accessible guide to discerning consumers. Consumer support for firms or countries that abide by approved standards can aid sales and incomes. Consumer boycotts or opprobrium have had an adverse impact on the profitability of the corporations involved. Where firms are sensitive to negative publicity, certification programmes such as the Fair Trade mark for sustainable production or the Kimberley Process Certification Scheme against conflict diamonds have been somewhat effective in yoking corporate practice to consumer concern.

The key to maximizing the effectiveness of these certification schemes lies in drawing simple conceptual links between consumer products and harmful practices lower down the production chain. The mining industry has seen some progress in this field in the last ten years. There is an incipient role for this sort of pressure in the energy industry, but it has not proved effective thus far in changing consumer behaviour other than around particular episodes, such as when the planned disposal of the Brent Spar oil-loading platform led to a boycott of Shell products, or more recently when BP suffered a consumer backlash following the explosion of its Deepwater Horizon oil platform in the Gulf of Mexico. The more commoditized the production (such as crude steel or bulk coal) and the greater its use as an input into another product, the less chance there is of harnessing public awareness to influence corporate behaviour.

The Hard End

While professional networks, corporations, research groups, and civil society pressure can go a considerable distance in addressing some global management challenges, there are many areas where this soft power is unlikely to be sufficient. Governments or corporations with entrenched interests often require more than soft power to alter their positions and abide by global rules. Some problems can only be solved through the hard power of legislation, and in these cases the involvement of nation states is unavoidable. Ideally, legislation addressing global problems, whether it is carbon-reduction targets or financial-sector regulation, would be introduced and implemented in a concerted worldwide effort. This would share the burdens equally, and avoid regulatory races to the bottom.

The uncertainties associated with systemic risks are in themselves reason for global action. To do nothing about climate change would be an imprudent gamble. Although the science is clear that climate change is man-made, we are not certain of its every effect; there are potentially unforeseen tipping points, such as the disruption of the Gulf Stream or gyrations in weather patterns, which would wildly skew our predictions. Even if the central view of climate scientists is perceived to be a net positive outcome for northern European countries, the range of possibilities includes numerous extremely negative outcomes. In addition, the second-order impacts need to be considered. Among these could be global instability, famine, and increased pressures for migration.

Humans are risk-averse, and our expectations of government are a function of this. Our primary demand should be that they safeguard us from ill—we do not expect them to conduct potentially disastrous gambles on our future.

This chapter has considered the potential of coalitions of willing countries, transnational networks, and business in facing today's challenges. To this list of powerful actors we must add the increasing power of the individual resulting from technological change and growing hyper-connectivity. Individuals can contribute in new ways to global solutions. Individuals now also pose a potentially unprecedented threat. It is to this we turn in Chapter 4.

CHAPTER FOUR

The Power of One: The Role of Individuals

Villains in the Village

The 21st century will be defined by the extent to which we are able to increase the power and effectiveness of global institutions, as connectivity introduces new global challenges and turns domestic issues into global coordination problems. Growing interconnectivity will bring dizzying demands on global institutions. Hyperconnectivity will also endow the individual with greater power than has ever been wielded. Individuals all over the globe will see their abilities to change the world amplified. This may be used to bring about good or ill.

If the world of the 21st century is a global village, then the village thugs have the power to wreak massive destruction. There are no village elders to stop them. The challenge of global governance this century will require the management of global threats posed not only by states but also by individuals. At the same time, the newly expanded power of individuals to initiate and propel positive change presents the opportunity for novel and creative solutions to global problems.

The factors that are complicating the institutional balance of forces simultaneously are globalizing the scope of individuals' power to effect change. Chapter 3 described how the once unitary sovereignty of states is being encroached upon by global institutions and new networks of professional bodies and civil-society activists. Empowered by new technological advances and today's hyper-connectivity, individuals are increasingly able to circumvent states and even to confront them directly. As the 11 September and other mass terrorist attacks demonstrate, actions that were once the exclusive domain of states, such as engagement in war, are now within the capability of individuals. We are no longer threatened only by the belligerence of enemy states. We are perhaps even more threatened by hostile individuals, who may reside within our societies, and even next door.

Yet an increasingly networked world has powerful advantages, not only in terms of our collective ability to develop and share ideas, but also to propagate and organize actions. As individuals, we can harness connectivity to amplify our voice, resulting in a greater ability to communicate with a disparate audience and a greater capacity to coordinate with like-minded activists. With national and global structures failing to grapple with today's challenges, there is an opportunity and a need for individuals all over the world to cooperate and influence global policy.

Examples already abound of the impacts that individuals can have beyond their national borders, in many cases influencing the global challenges that are the focus of this book. The financial sector has proved highly vulnerable to individuals who, through unauthorized, ill-monitored, and risky trading practices, have brought established banks to their knees. Now the subject of a Hollywood film and several books, Nick Leeson was a rogue trader who was singlehandedly responsible for the demise of his employer, Barings Bank, the UK's oldest investment bank, in 1995. In 2008 Jérôme Kerviel engaged in rogue trading through his apparent mastery of computing programes at Société Générale that led to an estimated loss of US$4.9 billion and a serious risk to the viability of the bank. More recently, in 2011 the Swiss bank UBS announced that it had lost over US$2 billion thanks to alleged unauthorized trading by Kweku Adoboli, the London-based director of the bank's Global Synthetic Equities Trading team.[86]

In 2012 JP Morgan Chase announced a loss of at least US$2 billion due to the 'London Whale' making risky trades on credit derivatives which subsequent reports suggest could cost the bank as much as US$9 billion.[87] The combination of excessive risk-taking and weak controls in a world of hyper-connected markets and technological wizardry not understood by senior managers means that months after the loss was first recognized uncertainty remains as to its actual impact. The problem has become so acute in finance that the profession has been contaminated in the minds of many citizens and politicians with the actions of toxic individuals.

Pandemics, by their nature, are passed on from individual to individual. Animal to human transmission is also a major concern, and has been at the root of the HIV/AIDS pandemic and recent avian and swine flu. The latter, for example, was transferred from a pig to a person in Mexico in early 2009. The pathogen spread rapidly, and is said to have caused at least 18,000 deaths. As discussed in Chapter 2, the growing ease by which individuals are able to acquire the necessary equipment and expertise to manufacture smallpox, Ebola, or even worse bio-pathogens and initiate devastating pandemics is a cause for increasing concern. The availability and affordability of equipment required to synthesize pathogens is growing at an alarming rate, along with the exponentially declining cost of DNA synthesis. Meanwhile, the publication of lethal 'recipes' grows exponentially with the Internet.

The cyberworld is one in which individuals may exercise global power. Individuals in their own home can expose and exploit the vulnerabilities of our interconnected, Internet-based society through vicious cyberattacks—with consequences far beyond their sitting rooms. In 2011, Ryan Cleary, a teenager from Essex, UK, was arrested in relation to attacks on the websites of America's CIA and the UK's Serious Organised Crime Agency (SOCA).[88] With a computer, Internet connection, and some IT ingenuity, an individual can cause significant harm to governments, businesses, as well as other individuals.

More positively, on the issue of climate change there has been a significant push in recent years for individuals to recognize their own contribution to global warming and to change their habits accordingly. Increasing public awareness about their carbon footprint has grown substantially, with information now featuring on food packaging, electronic goods, flower baskets, and plane tickets. People can now access government 'carbon calculators' for advice on how to calculate, avoid, reduce, and offset their own carbon emissions.[89]

Energy efficiency in our homes is another area where individuals are making a difference—through solar panels, water tanks, improved insulation, and other greener technologies—while electronic cars and initiatives such as city-bike schemes also encourage individuals to change their behaviour for the sake of the planet.

A key challenge in the area of climate change is for these ideas to become contagious so that they become the norm rather than the exception. They also need to be translated into national action, with commitments binding countries to reductions in greenhouse gases, support for technology transfer, and other vital actions. The transmission between individual choice and collective action is the weak link.

Migration is an intensely personal activity, in the sense that it is individuals who migrate and make the brave decisions to leave their homes in search of a better life. In *Exceptional People* (2011) my co-authors and I show that the decision to migrate is typically undertaken in consultation with relatives and friends, and the benefits are often remitted to others, but it is individuals who make the necessary sacrifices. We analyse how migrants benefit their host societies by providing a source of economic and social dynamism and growth.

However, these benefits may not be shared immediately by host communities and workers, who may come to regard migrants as more of a threat than an opportunity. The trade-offs between the local and short-term dislocation and wider and longer-term societal gains is at times a source of acute tension. If not effectively managed, these issues can translate into politically expedient policies which place increasing control over migrants at the cost of the long-term dynamism of society. Previous chapters have identified the failure of global governance to address key migration issues. Countries prefer to act in a unilateral manner when it comes to matters of migration. Not surprisingly perhaps, migration is the orphan of the international system. In this area, as in climate change, developing a more rational response at the global level requires the transmission of individual concerns into policies at the national and global level which are more closely aligned with the needs of global society.

All politics in the end is local. The growing power of individuals means that this phrase, which is almost a truism, may be extended to 'politics is about individuals'. Certainly, the power of individuals in terms of creating both problems and solutions relating to global governance is rising. This power, if harnessed creatively for good, can be instrumental and transformative. The previous chapter explored the role of transnational networks, the private sector, and other informal, more creative, collaborations as part of our potential armoury in the development of 21st-century governance.

In this chapter we consider the potential of the individual. I draw inspiration from technological innovation as well as examples drawn from politics, responses to disasters, and other areas of individual action.

The Technology Revolution

Technological change has for millennia been associated with massive leaps in living standards—from the taming of fire and the domestication of animals to more recent advances in the discovery of drugs, computing, and Internet networks. To stand in the way of technological progress is to stand in the way of development and poverty reduction.

Over the last century average life expectancy has increased by over thirty years. Income has increased a hundredfold in some countries.[90] Productivity has been steadily growing, allowing us to work less and earn more. All of these changes have greatly improved our lives. Accelerated globalization offers an opportunity to build upon these successes, spreading education and facilitating innovation which should benefit us all.

The ability of the Internet to facilitate communication and collaboration between like-minded individuals is a new development. From humble beginnings in the 1950s alongside the development of computers, the Internet continues to grow exponentially in complexity, power, and reach (see Figure 11). We are increasingly dependent on the services it provides and—from banking to cloud computing, social networking to grocery shopping—the Internet pervades every aspect of day-to-day life.

The Internet carries the potential to greatly enhance the lives of individuals across the world. Many millions of individuals now have access to online educational resources that were previously available

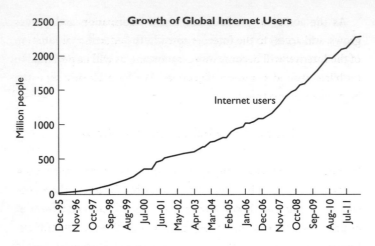

FIGURE 11 Growth of Internet users

only to small minorities in the richest of countries. Lectures and texts are distributed over the Internet, often free of charge. In 2001, the Massachusetts Institute of Technology stunned some education observers by announcing it would publish all educational materials from its courses freely on the Internet. Within ten years, this leading institution has shared materials from more than 2,000 courses with approximately 100 million people. Collaborative communities on sites such as Wikipedia and YouTube have created vast pools of resources for the autodidact. Creative projects such as Galaxy Zoo are enabling academics to leverage public interest on key research questions by recruiting the help of tens or even hundreds of thousands of volunteers.[91] These armies of volunteers have helped search for new galaxies, studied the lives of the Ancient Greeks, and searched temperature records from ancient ships' logs for climate research.

As the ability to produce and share information and images grows, and access to the Internet spreads, the educational function of the Internet will become more important, as will its potential to mobilize around common objectives. We have already seen the beginnings of this trend.

The Software Behind the Hardware

Internet access was for many years too niche for large communities to form online, and bandwidth was too slow for much sharing to take place. Large-scale collaboration was mostly limited to groups of programmers who had the expertise to make the most of the Internet. Subsequently, the Internet has enabled a blossoming of collaboration and the establishment of truly global networks of research. Furthermore, the Internet has created a generation of programmers who are often self-taught, and share strong norms encouraging free distribution and development. There is strong support for communal learning, with programmers offering each other advice and guidance. As a result, these communities have created free tools that at times are superior to commercial products. For instance, around two-thirds of websites use a web server called Apache, developed for free distribution by an open community of programmers.[92] Millions of individuals use an operating system called Ubuntu, which is not only provided for free but comes packaged with an extensive suite of open-source software.[93]

More generally, both the personal computer and the Internet are supremely flexible tools, and this flexibility is their greatest strength. Any skilled individual can create code and distribute it over the Internet for little or no cost. The Internet itself places no restrictions on the content of data transferred between networked computers, and does not discriminate between different sources and types of data. The result is a constant stream of new programes and Internet sites, originating from hobbyists, enthusiasts, and entrepreneurs. This process is responsible for much of the growing functionality of personal computers—innovations ranging from Skype to Wikipedia have grown out of this flexibility.[94]

Genius Unlocked

As Internet access becomes more common and bandwidth grows, individuals are increasingly able to share video, music, and other media. We should expect the sort of collaboration already common among the programming community to spread. The combination of rapid rises in educational attainment and literacy with global connectivity provides an unprecedented potential for drawing in individuals around the world to engage in innovation and problem-solving. In recent decades, illiteracy around the world has fallen from around 50 per cent to close to 20 per cent, and educational attainment has leapt ahead as hundreds of millions of young people gain secondary and tertiary education for the first time. The combination of these leaps forward in the ability to gain and mobilize knowledge with new collaborative tools facilitated by the Internet heralds a new era in connectivity and collaboration.

This is a step-change rather than an incremental change. The heightened potential and enlarged size of collaborative communities, and the ease with which they can communicate and draw a worldwide audience, has established a new creative cauldron to accelerate the formation of skills and ideas. Chris Anderson, curator of Technology, Entertainment and Design (conference and website), calls this phenomenon 'crowd-accelerated innovation': as the size of a crowd grows, the likelihood that they will generate radical innovation increases exponentially.[95] By joining up similarly interested individuals, the web creates a hotbed of experimentation and exploration with the potential to yield enormous returns.

There are dangers associated with such innovations—individuals can now create powerful deadly pathogens, collapse banks, or subvert the Internet. Crowd-accelerated innovation is the other side of the same coin. The development of the Internet has coincided with the age of accelerated globalization, following the fall of the Berlin Wall and ideological and economic opening. Not only has the number of connected participants multiplied exponentially, but their level of understanding and ability to engage has simultaneously risen. The number of connected people matters greatly, especially if they have the basic or advanced education to be able to absorb and contribute to innovation and ideas.

The period of hyper-connectivity over the past two decades is also one I characterize as being 'genius unlocked'. This is in the literal sense, in terms of the number of exceptionally smart people around the world who have become educated and connected for the first time, including from the slums of Sao Paolo, Soweto, Mumbai, or Shanghai. I also mean genius unlocked in the figurative sense. Even though the overwhelming majority of individuals who are connected are not actually geniuses, the collective outcome of their collaboration can be radically different and as if a team of geniuses had applied themselves.

Technological Possibilities

The Internet allows us to mobilize the work of many thousands of scientists, or the opinions of many millions of social activists. The IPCC, for example, brings together scientists from 195 countries to assess the scientific, technical, and socioeconomic information regarding climate change, with much of this activity taking place through online communities.

It is now commonplace that anyone with a computer can publish their most trivial thoughts to a global audience. With the Internet revolution, the costs of information production and distribution have plummeted and are negligible. In this sense, the individual's ability to broadcast their own view of the world has expanded remarkably. Individuals with specialist and insider knowledge have suddenly found that they can broadcast their insights and secrets— this turns everyone into a potential reporter and enriches the global information pool. Before the Internet, newspapers had a correspondent for every country at best; now, we have potential correspondents in every town, city, and institution.

Digital Democracy

An example of the influence of such citizen journalism is reflected in the South Korean website, OhMyNews. Established in 2000, with the motto 'every citizen is a reporter', this pioneer of online citizen journalism proved an important influence on the outcome of the 2002 South Korean election. Roh Moo Hyun won the presidency by a narrow margin, thanks to an eleventh-hour online campaign to rally young voters. With continuous updates in the closing hours as controversy surrounded Roh Moo Hyun's opponent, the site attracted over 720,000 hits in just ten hours. Upon victory, Hyun's first presidential interview went to OhMyNews, and he is commonly referred to as the 'world's first internet president'.[96]

Beyond citizen journalism, online resources are fundamentally challenging our politicians and government structures in other ways—with both positive and negative implications. In November 2009, someone with access to the US Department of Defence's SIPRNet leaked around 250,000 US diplomatic cables to whistle-blower website WikiLeaks. One year later, WikiLeaks published online the collection of cables from US embassies between 1966 and 2010, shedding unprecedented light on the inner workings both of American foreign policy and of the states it supports and tolerates around the world.

WikiLeaks is part of an important movement of network-powered politics, charged by the individual—fighting for more transparency and accountability within powerful institutions such as governments. Since its establishment in 2006, this non-profit online media organization has published, for example, over 6,500 Congressional Research Service Reports (typically only available to Congress); won an Amnesty Award for its reports on corruption and human rights abuses in Kenya; provided details on Barclays Bank's tax payments; and homed in on the operations of the Church of Scientology.[97]

In 2008, an individual whistleblower in Peru was able to publish, through WikiLeaks, a recording of a vice-president of state-owned Petroperú, Alberto Quimper, and lobbyist Rómulo Léon, discussing bribes in exchange for favouring Norwegian petroleum company Discover when awarding exploration rights.[98] The ensuing scandal resulted in the resignation of Prime Minister Jorge del Castillo.[99]

The same interconnectivity which puts us in danger from individuals beyond our own state's protective reach also allows us to outmanoeuvre and expose states which seek to pursue private interests at public expense. Such transparency is crucial if valued norms are to be established and upheld. Without our global communication network, it would have been extremely difficult for the whistleblower to bring the documents to the attention of so wide an audience, and it is precisely because they could reach so broad an audience that the new information could become a catalyst for regime change.

Shifting Power: The Arab Spring

A striking recent example of the power of the individual to spread information and mobilize others for change can be found in the Arab Spring of 2011. The revolutions of Tunisia and Egypt led to the dramatic toppling of authoritarian regimes in those countries and inspired challenges to established patterns across the Arab world. It is difficult to predict how and when these rippling storms will subside, but as Kemal Dervis, vice-president of the Brookings Institution argues, 'one thing is certain: there is no turning back'.[100] New social and political movements, charged by ordinary individuals rather than political or even religious leaders, are challenging the structures and power systems across the Middle East and North Africa.

It is possible to pinpoint the individuals who helped trigger the revolutions in both Tunisia and Egypt. Mohamed Bouazizi, a college-educated street vendor, immolated himself in December 2010 in protest at rife corruption, inequality, unemployment, and censorship in Tunisia. Despite Tunisia's strict web controls, Bouazizi's drastic act rapidly spread through social media tools. Large-scale protests, organized through informal online networks, rapidly formed, while others used social media to share stories of state oppression, police brutality, and unrest. By mid-January 2011, over 300,000 videos had been placed on YouTube tagged 'Sidi Bouzid', the town in which Bouazizi set himself alight.[101] The twenty-three-year rule of President Zine el-Abidine Ben Ali collapsed within a month, and a statue now stands in Sidi Bouzid in remembrance of the one man whose actions unleashed a protest movement that would reshape the Arab World.[102]

In Egypt, the turning point came in the case of a young businessman from Alexandria, Khaled Said, who was reportedly beaten to death in 2010 by two police officers. Public outrage was quickly channelled towards a Facebook page, cleverly titled 'We are All

Khaled Said', which was to become a rallying call for opposition to state brutality and abuse.

Recognizing the potential power of increasing public frustration, a prominent student blogger named 'Kamel' and a Google executive and administrator of the Facebook page, Wael Ghomin, joined forces to plan Egypt's landmark first day of protest—'The Day of Rage'—on 25 January 2011. This online campaign brought together hundreds of thousands of activists in Cairo, Alexandria, and Damanhur to protest against President Hosni Mubarak's oppressive thirty-year rule. Facebook and Twitter enabled demonstrators to access update information about further events, participants, and leaders. One event saw 90,000 people confirm their attendance via social media tools which both inspired others to participate but also demonstrated the solidarity and scale of the protests.[103] Internet-savvy protestors continued posting blogs, photos, tweets, and videos, calling for more and more Egyptians to join them. The protests lasted eighteen days before Mubarak's regime dramatically collapsed.

Social media is not responsible for these uprisings, but it clearly played a key role in accelerating events through the speedy transmission and exchange of information, and mobilizing citizens, outside of the state's control. The youthful profile of these Arab states, where the median age of the population is around 26, ten years below the median age in the US, Europe, or China, may have also been a factor, not least in their willingness to turn to new technologies and social media.

We must be cautious, however, because the inspiring examples of Egypt (median age 24) and Tunisia (30) have not transpired in all countries. Social media played little role in the bloody downfall of Muammar Gaddafi in Libya (median age 24). At the time of writing, the Arab Spring seems closer to a dark, cold winter in places like Syria (median age 22) and Yemen (18), where conflicts between

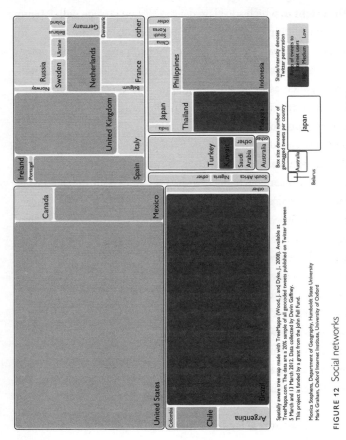

Spatially aware tree map made with TreeMappa (Wood, J. and Dyke, J. 2008). Available at
TreeMappa.com. The data are a 20% sample of all geocoded tweets published on Twitter between
5 March and 13 March 2012. Data collected by Devin Gaffney.
This project is funded by a grant from the John Fell Fund.

Monica Stephens, Department of Geography, Humboldt State University
Mark Graham, Oxford Internet Institute, University of Oxford

FIGURE 12 Social networks

M. Graham and M. Stephens, 'A Geography of Twitter', Oxford Internet Institute, June 2012.

governments, the military, and civilians have cost many lives. The significance and ultimate results of the Arab Spring will no doubt be analysed and debated for years to come, but the role of empowered individuals will be central to the story.

The extent to which social media can sustain change will depend on the translation of virtual communities into organizations and structures that can exercise political power and sustain change. Without such sustained structure, the waves of engagement on social networks, such as depicted in Figure 12, can quickly collapse and give way to new waves which may ripple across and dissipate the mobilizing force of the Internet. The transformation of the waves of protest associated with the Arab Spring into an uneven series of stuttering political reforms reflects the difficulties associated with web-based movements being carried through to political change.

The potential for citizens to inform is evident in Syria where, despite the best attempts of the regime to hide its crimes, video images taken with mobile phones are uploaded and transmitted. Some find their way into the global news, with CNN and other channels providing testimony to the suffering on the ground. The power of every individual to capture and transmit information creates the potential for a new age of transparency and accountability. This cannot be simply mapped into assumptions regarding sustained change in political structures and processes, but it does nevertheless mark a significant step forward in the potential for individual citizens to shape national and global priorities.

Natural Disasters and the Digital Age

Beyond the political domain, social media and technology are also fundamentally changing the speed and agility with which individuals and countries can respond to natural disasters. When the Haiti earthquake struck, Crisis Commons initiated a worldwide project whereby volunteers could collaborate to compile a map of Haiti from satellite images. Within less than two weeks they had created 'the most complete digital map of Haiti's roads, hospitals, triage centers and refugee camps currently available'. 'Before all you could do was send money to the Red Cross', says Noel Dickover, co-founder of Crisis Commons, 'Now we've figured out a way to bring the average citizen, literally around the world, to come and help in a crisis'.[104] It has never been easier to contribute to global knowledge and problem-solving.

With each successive recent natural disaster—Hurricane Katrina, the earthquakes in Haiti, Chile, and New Zealand, and the earthquake and tsunami in Japan—the role of social media has increased significantly. According to Twitter analysis, the use of that social media platform increased by 500 per cent in Japan at the time of the devastating earthquake, as family and friends reached out to each other in the moments immediately after the quake. It then became a vital tool in the proactive organization and dissemination of information about the crisis, the availability of food and other support services, radiation advice, as well as coordinating donations. Google now also hosts a 'Crisis Response Centre' that aims to help make critical information more available during crisis situations or disasters.[105] Such tools are shifting the control of information and updates from a few major organizations, such as the government, major NGOs, or traditional media sources, to allow the power of multiple voices, and often individuals, to emerge.

The Flip Side

Not all acceleration and broadening of the means of communication is beneficial—the ability to spread information is also an ability to spread misinformation, whether knowingly or not. If the Internet's communicative potential is to be fully reaped, we must find mechanisms to filter out the enlightening from the misleading. The problem is digital deluge and selectivity. How are we to distinguish between fraudulent or accurate sources and how are we to know where to look? To drink from the fire hydrant we need new trusted tools that identify our needs and provide only the required content for our consumption. Intermediaries, or trusted networks, become vital conduits of information.

The importance of this is especially visible in the current financial system, where nervous stock markets are susceptible to the phenomenon George Soros calls 'reflexivity'. This is the propensity of individuals to form feedback loops, where enthusiasm or panic develops a self-fulfilling momentum of its own, and in which individual behaviour becomes that of the herd. This is associated with irrational exuberance and also catastrophic collapses in stock markets—the blowing and bursting of bubbles.[106]

In such circumstances, the slightest rumour about a company's stability can cause investors to flee precipitously and simultaneously, fearing less the truth of the rumour than that others will believe it— and so the prophesy becomes self-fulfilling. Société Générale,

> France's second-largest bank...was almost driven out of business in August 2011 thanks to rumours that it was on the brink of collapse. The origin of the claim were quotes from an anonymous source in the Mail on Sunday newspaper that the bank was in a 'perilous' state and 'on the brink of collapse'.[107]

After Société Générale lost 22.5 per cent of its value in one day, the newspaper was obliged to apologize; it seems likely that the journalist may have mistaken a fictional account of a crisis, published on the Internet by Le Monde, for fact.[108]

Without better mechanisms to filter good information from bad, the individual's ability to spread information will not retain its potency. Similarly, as we become increasingly reliant on the Internet to conduct our daily lives, protecting individual privacy and personal information on the Internet is critical. Public debates about national identity cards and other electronic tools aimed at providing a central point through which to connect with government services and other providers are hamstrung by public mistrust of the ability of government agencies to protect personal information. The recent case of the hacker who breached the website of Britain's largest abortion clinic and threatened to release all the names of the women who had used this service highlights the vulnerabilities we face in our increasingly online identity and the darker side of technological connectivity.

Online Identity

The Internet does not in fact tend towards anonymity, as might appear to be the case—compared with the obscurity of the offline grapevine, it offers a greater opportunity to trace rumours to their sources. Our statements can be tied to a virtual identity, and that virtual identity can bear a reputation which reflects the accuracy of the statements over time. This identity can form a robust foundation for sorting trustworthy from untrustworthy sources, which should temper the danger that comes with instantaneous communication.

A tweet stays forever on one's Twitter feed, stamped with its author's name, waiting to be quoted back years later. Websites such as eBay and Wikipedia rely on online identities to establish trust between users, and this works precisely because users can check their interlocutor's identity. Social networking sites such as Facebook are attempting to gather our various online presences into one identity, reinforcing the trust effect and further enabling audiences to discern the reliability of their informant. Recently launched Google+ has gone a step further with its 'real name policy', bridging the gap between online and offline identities and asking its users to prove their identity by scanning their government IDs, in the belief that this enhances online civility. It remains to be seen whether users will accept this constraint.[109]

Networking sites all rely on the advantages they offer—the ability to trade, to edit encyclopaedia articles, or to interact socially over the Internet—to convince users that it is worth their while to give up the radical anonymity of Web 1.0. This works well in the limited domains these websites offer—trading, factual authority, social interaction—but it only fences off abuse, it does not eliminate it and cannot fully prevent cyberaggression or criminals from entering trusted communities.

Global Problems, Individual Solutions

Individuals' increased power in the age of networks goes further than the ability to disseminate information. It may even present a way to facilitate action on key global challenges, including those that are the focus of this book, that goes beyond the rigid and seemingly antiquated structures of national governments or global institutions.

Where serious interests are at stake, states act in what they perceive to be the short-term interests of their citizens. Their actions are influenced by their political and other biases as well as media and lobbying. National identity remains the most powerful force. Politicians are adept at focusing on issues which resonate on the national stage. There is some evidence that growing familiarity with other cultures through travel, social networks, and media coverage may well be expanding our circles of empathy, and that a growing number of citizens feel they have a transnational identity, not least if they are migrants or the children of migrants.

In addition to increasing migration and travel, the social networks and media serve to raise awareness that at times transcends borders. One might mock the authenticity, or at least the efficacy, of manifestations of global fellowship when they amount to joining a Facebook group or tweeting expressions of solidarity, such as in the case of Western supporters of the Burmese protests of 2007 or the Iranian Green Revolution of 2009. Yet information and communication technology is clearly having an impact in terms of a heightened awareness of suffering around the world, and a growing commitment to global solidarity.

When the Haiti earthquake struck in January 2010, for example, worldwide empathy led to an estimated US$2.5 billion in aid given and a further US$1.3 billion pledged.[110] Within a week of the Tōhoku earthquake in Japan, donations were pledged by individuals residing in over one hundred countries, including over US$1 million from Azerbaijan to almost US$7 million in financial and food support from Thailand.[111] Often generosity came from distant individuals with no historical ties with Japan. Their urge to assist the victims of the earthquake and its aftermath sprang from a sense of common awareness and humanity. Shared responsibility, together with an increasing ease of action—in this case e-giving—is surely a consequence of our growing sense of interdependence and individual power to act.

Much has been written about the viral success of Kony 2012, a twenty-eight-minute film, produced by a small US charity called Invisible Children, which aims to highlight the plight of children in Uganda at the hands of the warlord, Joseph Kony. The film has been downloaded over 100 million times on YouTube, drawing unprecedented attention to a controversial issue that other human rights organizations, government agencies, and charities have been working on for years while barely scratching the surface in terms of public awareness.

The organization and film have received significant criticism for oversimplification, misinformation, and questions of financial accountability. The Ugandan Government has even responded with its own nine-minute film in response, correcting misinformation as Joseph Kony and his army are no longer based in Uganda. Despite such controversies, the Kony 2012 campaign and Invisible Children should be credited with igniting a global debate on the issue and inspiring millions of individuals, particularly young people, to get involved and take action in demanding answers from their national governments and global agencies such as the UN. Despite the rapid collapse of the wave of support, from which important lessons may also be drawn, the scale and speed with which Invisible Children was able to raise awareness has set new expectations regarding the potential power of social media.

From Soft to Hard Campaigns

If powerful interests are vested in the resolution of a particular collective action problem, as is the case with energy companies and climate change, states will be extremely slow to coordinate a solution. Individuals have the capacity to act as a counterweight to this inertia. Using the power of new information channels to communicate and spread information, individuals can form transnational pressure groups and give voice to the public interest by exerting their own pressure. Unlike private-sector lobbying, public pressure thrives on transparency and inclusive networks, and so it is these aspects of technological connectivity that must be accentuated.

The Make Poverty History and Live8 campaigns in 2005 succeeded in extracting some policy concessions from G8 governments by orchestrating a movement that spanned continents and grabbed the world's attention. Yet, a review of these campaigns reveals that grassroots movements may only go so far—once the press spotlight had faded, the politicians were slow to deliver on their promises, and found ways to minimize the commitments they had made. ONE's DATA report on the G7's delivery on the pledges made at the 2005 Gleneagles summit reveals that 'the G7 delivered only 61 per cent of their promised increases to sub-Saharan Africa by 2010', falling US$7 billion short.[112]

Although part-time activists find it easier to coordinate, helped by the phenomenon Clay Shirky calls 'ridiculously easy group forming', effective political activism requires stronger monitoring capabilities, and broad interest groups find it difficult to maintain the focus on key actors long enough to see reform carried through.[113] In the face of intransigent states, the capacity of soft people power to translate aspirations into sustained actions should not be overestimated.

In some areas, people power can take on a 'harder' character. When MasterCard, under pressure from the US government, suspended its banking services to WikiLeaks, it was targeted as part of hacktivist group Anonymous's Operation Avenge Assange. This took the form of a Distributed Denial of Service (DDoS) attack, but in contrast with the usual maliciously destructive variant, in which the attacker creates a botnet by possessing the computers of unsuspecting owners via malware and employs it for pure entertainment or financial gain, Operation Avenge Assange involved members of Anonymous choosing to download software to their own computers to create a 'voluntary botnet' for a political purpose. This globally coordinated group of individuals did not opt for the soft-power approach of the 2005 G8-focused campaigns. Through their creative use of computer networks, these hacktivists were able to generate a virtual form of hard power—forcing the MasterCard site to shut down—in retaliation against the US government's own exertion of pressure. John Walker, chief technology officer at cybersecurity company Secure Bastion, argues that 'this proves without question the power at people's fingertips'.[114]

This raises worrying questions about the accountability of such groups. Recently, for example, Anonymous attacked the website of the US Court of Appeals for the Ninth Circuit for believing that the group's tactics are 'cyber-terrorism'.[115] The group also has attacked the UK Government on the basis of its decision to deny Julian Assange safe passage from the Ecuadorian Embassy in London where he was granted political asylum.

Whatever one's views about the merits of the case or the associated actions, they demonstrate the possibility of individuals organizing to take action themselves in novel and at times effective ways rather than relying on traditional forms of protest or political parties or governments to take action on their behalf.

Combinations of institutional and individual response may also become increasingly powerful. For example, in January 2012 Wikipedia blacked out its English-language sites in protest against proposed legislation in the US—the Stop Online Piracy Act (SOPA) and the Protect IP Act (PIPA)—that, if passed, Wikipedia believed 'would seriously damage the free and open internet'.[116]

During the twenty-four-hour blackout of its own content, the Wikipedia page about SOPA and PIPA was accessed more than 162 million times, over eight million Americans looked up their elected representative's contact details, and the issue immediately began trending globally on Twitter. After Wikipedia and several other popular websites converted their home pages into virtual protest banners, the rapid mobilization of citizens and the prospect of further campaigns quickly led to a dropping of the planned legislative programme, scoring a quick triumph for action by a virtual community. In a signal of the growing power of online political activism, Senator Harry Reid, the majority leader in the US Congress, announced via Twitter that the vote on the controversial bill would be delayed.[117]

The virtual community will no doubt result in greater power for individuals to mobilize through networks which support particular causes. Equally, they can wreck the reputation of individuals, companies, or products, and create herding and hysteria. Their effectiveness in penetrating hard power remains weak. Mass mobilization against the regime of Bashar al-Assad has failed to shift the resolve of the Syrian regime and appears to have had only a limited impact on its Russian and Chinese supporters. While the immense power of the Internet provides new possibilities for virtual mobilization, its limitations and potentially destructive impacts need to be recognized.

Virtual Destruction

The enhanced ability to coordinate fosters not only opportunities but dangerous possibilities. While new technologies can be used to coordinate individuals to promote freedom of speech and democracy, they can also be employed to destructive ends. Like any form of power, their potential to contribute to the solutions and not to the problems depends on the intentions and skill of those who wield them.

In 2009, for example, thousands of private emails between climate scientists at the University of East Anglia's (UEA) Climate Research

Unit were hacked into and published online. The intention of those responsible was to distort and undermine the global debate on climate change on the eve of the critical UN IPCC meetings in Copenhagen. The controversy surrounding the emails gave a stronger voice to individuals, organizations, and politicians who dispute the scientific evidence around global warning, fuelling unhelpful and dangerous scepticism on one of today's biggest challenges.

While independent reviews have criticized the UEA scientists for their reluctance to share data and open up their research to greater scrutiny, the evidence for global warming is unquestionable. It is no coincidence that the next tranches of email leaks occurred one week before the major round of climate talks in Durban in 2011. In this case, technology enabled individuals to undermine and distract at a critical time for a vitally important negotiation.

During the London riots of August 2011, social media such as Twitter, Facebook, and especially the encrypted BlackBerry Messaging, were used to great effect by gangs of rioters. Thanks to these techniques of coordinated destruction, Home Secretary Theresa May said the rioters were always 'one step ahead of the police', successively appearing in one location to loot and then dispersing as soon as the police arrived with unprecedented rapidity.[118] This connectivity was also instrumental in the viral spread of the riots to other cities in England. Conversely, social media was helpful in some respects—with commuters and other citizens using the tools for up-to-date information during the unrest regarding which areas to avoid, as well as for transport updates. Mass clean-up campaigns were subsequently coordinated via Twitter and Facebook, such as the locally organized @riotcleanup group which attracted over 70,000 followers.[119]

Yet the balance of power between those who use networks to coordinate action and those who monitor their communications with the objective of disrupting that coordination is delicate. The Iranian Green Revolution of 2009 was nicknamed the 'Twitter Revolution' because protesters coordinated protests through social media. As time unfolded, however, events in Iran might more appropriately have been named the 'Twitter Repression', because it was precisely through social media that the Iranian authorities were able to track the ring leaders and bring them to trial. Such tactics are not solely the domain of authoritarian regimes. A similar reaction to the London riots may have taken place, with BlackBerry's maker Research in Motion pledging to assist police in pinpointing rioters, and with two men being sentenced to four years in prison for setting up Facebook groups to coordinate rioting.[120]

There is a balance to be struck between overcoming our vulnerability to hostile groups who can outsmart police with technology, on the one hand, and our willingness to allow law enforcement to interfere with the privacy of citizens in their bid to stay abreast of developments, on the other hand. The British Prime Minister's threat to suspend social network sites to prevent them being used by rioters contrasted with the British Government's protest against the Egyptian authorities' attempts to shut down the mobile networks during the riots in Egypt. While technically the potential to shut off networks certainly exists, in practice since they are so destabilizing for business and society in general, anything but a short-term deliberate switching off of the web is unlikely.

Good and Bad Networks

Connectivity does not only contribute to the individual's ability to communicate, whether to inform or to coordinate—it also provides the individual with a broader ability to affect others through their actions. Increasing connectivity means that in many aspects of our lives we rely on networks that span the globe. This is on balance a tremendously beneficial development, for it extends the possibilities open to us in our daily lives, from when we can eat particular food to where we choose to work. Yet this global reach also raises our vulnerability as it exposes us to others and increases our interdependence.

Of greatest concern, new technologies grant a single person or small group the ability to affect great numbers of people with one judiciously targeted attack. Although not malicious, the devastating effect of the actions of rogue traders who sidestep their bank's trading limits, such as Nick Leeson or Jérôme Kerviel, demonstrates the damage that can be inflicted when the taut rules of our systems are disobeyed. They may not have intended to damage the institutions they worked for, but the effect of their actions demonstrates the destructive power our connectivity grants the individual. Whether by design or accident, individuals have a new-found ability to shape all our lives for better or for worse.

From food supply chains to the Internet, the further our essential networks stretch, the more immediately we are vulnerable to hostile action by individuals outside our state's jurisdiction. A pickpocket can only target their immediate neighbours, but a hacker can plant a Trojan horse in computers on the other side of the world.

Our networks have grown from the demand that information, goods, and people are able to circulate with global range. It was thanks to our advanced transport and communications technologies that a search-and-rescue team from Iceland could arrive in Haiti within twenty-four hours of the 2010 earthquake, and personnel from over twenty countries within two days.[121] Yet the same connectivity which is used by most to expand the sphere of their trade and communication can also be used by hostile individuals to extend the reach of their malicious aims; a bio-pathogen released at an international transport hub could spread across the globe within days.[122]

In September 2001, envelopes containing anthrax were sent to the offices of several media organizations and two US Senators, resulting in the deaths of five people. The connectivity of the postal system unwittingly served to propagate the attack. Individuals can use our usually beneficial supply and transport networks to distribute harm to a greater number of potential victims—this destructive activity does not target connectivity itself but instead harnesses it to its own ends.

The terrorist cult Aum Shinrikyo have tried and failed several times to cause widespread pain and death by releasing pathogens in Japan. Most famously, in March 1995 members of the group punctured bags containing liquid Sarin nerve gas on several Tokyo metro trains in the middle of rush hour. In May 1995, other members attempted to release hydrogen cyanide through the ventilation system of Tokyo's busiest train station, Shinjuku. In each case disastrous fatalities were avoided by sheer chance—fortunately Aum Shinrikyo had hurriedly produced a low-lethality batch of Sarin and the hydrogen cyanide release mechanism was discovered and extinguished before it could detonate.[123] If the attacks had succeeded, deaths could have reached the hundreds of thousands. The pathogens, strategically placed at vital nodes, would have harnessed Tokyo's reliance on its public transport network to reach and harm as many people as possible. Our vulnerability on a global scale derives from the same characteristic: the very same systems that deliver us so much good can be manipulated to serve as vectors of harm.

Of particular concern is that our increasing connectivity is combining with technological capability and knowledge reaching more and more people at a pace that is far ahead of the regulatory or state capacity to monitor or control its dissemination and implications. Malicious individuals can exploit connectivity in a further way, not harnessing it but destroying connectivity itself. The systemic nature of our essential networks exposes us to the targeted destruction of a crucial node. A cyberattack on the servers of one frequently used service such as PayPal can thus affect millions of users across the world. Sea pirates, of whom an estimated 1,500 to 3,000 operate off the coast of Somalia, also thrive on the globalized world's connectivity. Our reliance on supply chains, which span the globe, provides them with the heavy shipping traffic through the Gulf of Aden from which they pick their victims. The cost of their activities to the world economy is estimated at between US$4.9 and US$8.3 billion for 2010 alone, and this does not count the less quantifiable but personally catastrophic harm of deaths and kidnapping.[124]

Our reliance on nodes in our nations or on the other side of the globe, whether Internet servers or financial centres, creates in itself a new type of vulnerability. In these cases individuals might not use our connection to a network to carry destruction into our homes, as in the case of bioterrorism, but they can threaten us by destroying something distant upon which we are vitally dependent. Connectivity is thus both a vehicle via which harm can be sent towards us, and a good whose destruction can be threatened.

Whether connectivity is used or targeted, it has become increasingly difficult for states to halt threats at our national border. Most importantly, networks allow attackers to launch their strikes from beyond the jurisdictional reach of the victim's state. The relative ease of access to the requisite technology only serves to compound this problem. A single individual can mount a DDoS attack using a single personal computer. More fundamentally, the networked nature of such attacks, with individuals remotely deploying botnets of computers conquered by means of viruses, means that 'most of the time it will be impossible for victims to ascertain the identity of the attacker'.[125] The equivalent is also the case for bioterrorism, as noted by the US Department of Homeland Security, given that biological weapons are easily concealed and hard to track. The threat of punishment possesses little deterrent effect in such circumstances.

Despite the dangers, the option of reversing connectivity is unpalatable. Too much of our prosperity and way of life depends on our global networks. Any solution must therefore attempt to reduce the risks while facilitating the benefits. Anyone who has travelled by air in the last decade knows the cost in terms of convenience and efficiency that is involved in securing a vital network. Similarly, solutions to sea pirates are readily available, including 'Secure-Ship, an electrified wire fence that delivers a 9,000-volt nonlethal shock to anyone attempting to climb aboard'; long-range acoustic devices capable of causing permanent damage to hearing from a distance of more than 300 metres, or simply having private armed teams aboard during passage through dangerous waters.[126]

The shipping industry on the whole does not invest in these defences, however, because the cost of the pirates' activities is too small as a proportion of the industry's revenue to make such investments worthwhile.[127] In a similar way, we may decide that we could counter terrorists with widespread phone-tapping or widespread distribution of bio-pathogen sensors. The financial costs and danger of giving such intrusive powers to law enforcement, with the possibility that they might one day abuse their powers, is currently judged to outweigh the benefit of the heightened security such technologies and capabilities may offer. This is unlikely to last, as devastating threats lead to new calls for heightened vigilance and protection.

The Power of One

Interconnectivity is granting individuals greater power to circumvent states and threaten society. The power of individuals to do harm, whether out of malice or for financial gain, and even by accident, will continue to rise rapidly in the coming decades. The geographical reach of individuals will widen as our networks provide a direct route to our homes, and the potency of any one attack will be magnified by our reliance on superconnected networks with vulnerable nodes. Our reliance on global networks renders us vulnerable to malicious individuals and undermines the ability of states to protect us. Even when the individuals act with less malicious motives, as in the case of activism, there is a worrying absence of accountability on their part.

Yet while connectivity puts us in greater danger by empowering our would-be aggressors, it simultaneously empowers individuals with positive and more benevolent aims. The ease of spreading information, if balanced with the right filtering mechanisms, offers great potential for global coordination and collaboration to solve problems and hold governments and international organizations to account. The harnessing of the positive power of individuals is vital to addressing the challenges of the 21st century.

CHAPTER FIVE

What Can Be Done?

Where to From Here?

In Chapter 1 I identified several major challenges to our increasingly interdependent global society. These threats cannot be tackled at a domestic and regional level. They have become global in scope and must therefore be addressed from a global perspective. Chapter 2 highlighted the fact that the existing institutions of governance are unfit for managing these issues of the global commons. Nations that jealously guard their narrow sovereign interests, and lumbering multilateral institutions such as the UN, World Bank, and IMF that are captured by out-of-date mandates and governed by divided nations, are not in a position to proactively address our global needs. The current arrangements were reasonably effective in dealing with the major challenges of the second half of the 20th century. However, they are ill-equipped to tackle the rapidly emerging and dynamic 21st-century challenges.

Globalization at Stake

In our increasingly hyper-connected world, local crises, which once would only have endangered one country, now threaten to engulf the entire global system. Recent examples include terror attacks that arose from Al Qaeda bases in Afghanistan, a global financial crisis cascading from the collapse of Lehman Brothers in New York, a swine flu pandemic fanning out from Mexico City, and escalating cyberattacks emanating from cyberspace.

In all these cases, even the most powerful countries were unable to safeguard their own territories. Some countries can pose a threat to the rest of the world by design. Increasingly, however, the systemic risks that threaten us arise due to benign neglect or accident. While the threats may come from belligerent or failed states, they are at least as likely to emanate from countries that are stable and developed, as was the case with swine flu from Mexico or the financial crisis from the US. Whether a nation state is unable to detect and quarantine emerging viruses, or fails to uncover and discourage risky market practices, its failures now have consequences not only for its own population but also for the entire international community.

Our vulnerability is most acute, as in the case of cascading financial crises, pandemics, or cyberaggression, when the threat is spread via our global networks. Globalization and increased integration is simultaneously the source of our greatest opportunities and threats. Global governance is required to ensure that we are able to harvest the upside potential and mitigate and limit the downside risks. Failure to do so will be associated with increasing systemic risk. This in turn will foster a political reaction against globalization. Integration will be viewed as the source of our weakness and globalization will become associated with vulnerability rather than strength and opportunity. The result will be that societies retreat into nationalism, protectionism, and xenophobia. The ensuing downward spiral of deglobalization would unravel many of the global gains of the past decades. Poor countries and poor people have the most to lose from systemic risk and a reverse in globalization. A reversal of globalization would lead to lower world growth, higher unemployment, and more instability in food, employment, and other markets. It would weaken the growing bonds between nations and citizens and make the resolution of critical global challenges even more difficult. A reversal of globalization would escalate rather than reverse the rise in systemic risk. Solutions for systemic risk go hand in hand with a more inclusive and carefully managed globalization rather than a rejection of it.

Coordination and Free Riding

The global nature of the threats we face presents an unwieldy coordination challenge, as even capable states, seeking to get away with the least sacrifice possible, free ride on the cooperative efforts of others. In the case of finance, a key cause of the financial crisis was the race to the bottom amongst regulators, with financial supervisors in New York and London, in particular, seeking to capture market share by reducing the burdens to financial firms located in their jurisdictions. Even after the crisis, governments are reluctant to commit to globally agreed rules, as is evident in the weak powers and absence of executive capability given to the Financial Stability Board and the failure of Eurozone finance ministers to agree rules which bind all members.

In the case of migration governance, the measures required for a more efficient and humane system, such as being able to access and exercise one's pensions and political rights wherever one is currently living, depend on nations acting in concert. In the case of climate change, as the struggle to reduce carbon emissions attests, virtually all states are attempting to free ride. We thus risk achieving the worst outcome globally, as carbon emissions rise inexorably.

This is despite the prerequisites for a comprehensive response being within our grasp. Reaching agreement on the distribution of burdens across states is a challenge independent of the feasibility of the actions required.

There is no all-encompassing cure for the failures of globalization. Each of the challenges we face is compounded to varying degrees by the complicating factors of systemic interdependency and the free-rider problem outlined above. Any solution to global governance will need to be able to address these.[128]

Challenges to Coordination

The failure of the Federal Reserve and regulators in the US to understand the extent to which Lehman Brothers acted as a critical node in derivatives trading provided a trigger for the financial collapse. Similarly, it would only take the belated detection and ineffective quarantine of a contagious and deadly pathogen in one connected country in the international system in order for it to threaten the rest of the world. The fact that other states would have been able to nip it in the bud does not shield them from it once the pandemic is under way. Once a state attains the capability to detect and quarantine novel pathogens, however, there are few perverse incentives discouraging it from doing so. Warding off future pandemics, therefore, depends primarily on addressing the detection and quarantine capabilities of those connected states that lack them. The equivalent is true of cybersecurity.

Foreseeing and mitigating financial crises, on the other hand, requires action on both the detection and regulatory fronts. As with pandemics, we need to improve our ability to detect the financial practices that are leading to crashes, because currently our institutions are not able to do so swiftly enough. The domain of finance illustrates that even highly advanced countries are threatened by global contagion—indeed, it is the most advanced economies that pose, and may be vulnerable to, the greatest financial risk.

Climate change, too, presents difficulties for the most advanced and therefore carbon-dependent economies. We do not currently have the capability for a zero-carbon economy. Each state seeks to shift the costly burden of emissions reduction to the others, with the result that even when targets are agreed upon they are not ambitious enough. Alternatively, states agree to targets but with heavy caveats—to be used as an excuse to wriggle out of commitments at the first opportunity. Achieving a zero-carbon economy is a shrinking ideal for many countries. In the UK, the Cameron–Clegg Government came to office in 2009 pledging to be 'the greenest government ever'. Yet in October 2011, the Chancellor George Osborne, when speaking to the Conservative Party Conference, put paid to such ambitions. In a rebuke to those calling for greater leadership, he said 'We're going to cut our carbon emissions no slower but also no faster than our fellow countries in Europe.'[129]

Global migration provides long-term benefits but may have short-term costs for both the receiving countries and sending countries. Current immigration policies are crafted without consideration for the long-term benefits of a coordinated global policy. Governments are under pressure from their populations to limit the extent of migration, primarily as a result of the experience of social dislocation it can produce. While governments make migration policy on the basis of political expediency and narrow national interests, the right to exercise one's social and political rights across borders—essential to a functional and humane international migration regime—is dependent on coordination between states. Yet such a set of arrangements would involve agreement on the distribution of burdens between states.

Vital questions require international resolution. For example, how are migrants defined, who is responsible for the health of migrants, and should pensions be payable in another country? These and other matters require international coordination, and yet there is no international organization with the authority to act and enforce policies on such pressing migration issues.

Globalization: The Problem and Solution

I have argued in previous chapters that the turbo-charged globalization of recent decades is the source of unprecedented progress, but that potentially it also harbours the seeds of its own destruction. The matter requires urgent attention if the remarkable progress of recent decades is to be sustained. There are two priorities.

First, to be sustainable globalization must be inclusive. It needs to address employment and equity, and poor people and poor countries cannot be left out.[130]

Second, there is a danger that globalization leads to the spreading of global harms more rapidly than global goods. The underbelly of globalization is systemic risk. It is vital that these are identified and mitigated, so that networks and connectivity do not become vectors for cascading failures. This would lead to people slamming the doors of globalization shut.

Fortunately, the very process of globalization increases the potential for management of global problems due to increased ability to collaborate and communicate. Ideological and political barriers are coming down at least as quickly as economic barriers, so that only in North Korea are citizens cut off from the Internet and the ideas that flow across all other borders.

It remains to be seen to what extent the common humanity, which was so quickly and widely expressed in solidarity for the victims of the earthquakes of Haiti and Japan, can be translated into new forms of global mobilization and governance. There has been much talk recently of a growth in 'global citizenship' and 'global society'. Such terms are often accompanied by a narrative that claims that borders are dissolving, that cultural differences are evaporating, and that the loyalties of individuals no longer belong to the state, but to humanity. These claims are often exaggerated. Individuals still identify primarily with their country, government, and fellow (national) citizens. But increased contact with people of different nationalities may well have brought more qualified gains: cultural understanding, awareness of the global issues, and a willingness to step beyond parochial national interests.

Rapid urbanization has been associated with the rapid growth of cities. Cities in many countries are taking over from national governments in terms of their leadership regarding critical 21st-century governance challenges. Big cities typically benefit most from globalization, but are also most vulnerable to systemic risks. Their individual and collective action—such as the C40 network of the world's megacities—can make a significant difference and potentially provide a vital building-block, but is not a substitute for national and global agreements.

In the past, global governance reforms followed from global tragedies. The terrible loss of human life and opportunity in the 20th century, associated with the two world wars, Spanish flu, and the Great Depression, produced fundamental changes in global governance. The acceleration of globalization, literacy, and communication in recent decades has, we may hope, produced new levels of awareness that could lead to more proactive engagement to prevent global crises. Whether our accumulated connectivity and experience has created fresh perspectives on global governance and an ability to transcend national borders remains the most critical question of our time.

Ethical concerns are rising around the world, with citizens increasingly finding the means to hold their governments, corporations, and societies to account for abusive practices. Ethical questions go to the heart of many of the global challenges identified in this book. For many, a failure of ethics in banking and finance lies at the root of the financial crisis. Ethical questions are central to matters of intergenerational justice, which lie at the heart of the challenge of climate change, and ethical questions are similarly central to discussions on migration.

Pascal Lamy has recently suggested that the deficit in global governance reflects a more fundamental lack of shared values between countries. He and others argue that it is consequently necessary to put ethics at the centre of debates on the future of global governance.[131]

Building with BRICS

Part of the relative success of the global governance system in the second half of the 20th century is attributable to the dominance of the US and its allies—Europe and Japan—in global affairs. While the UN was stuck in a Cold War stalemate, the Bretton Woods institutions and others were dominated by the G7, or what cynics referred to as G1 given the US's dominant role. The past two decades have seen the doubling of incomes every eight years in China and robust growth in the other BRICS (Brazil, Russia, India, China, and, with the 'S' finally added in 2010, South Africa). The financial crisis has accelerated the longer-term decline in the G7 countries' ability to provide global leadership. The fundamental reason for this is the declining share of the G7 in the global economy. Led by the BRICS, the other 202 countries in the world have become more assertive on the subjects that matter to them, ranging from the small islands on climate change to cybersecurity in China.

The US, Europe, and Japan are financially bankrupt, with leaders across the board fighting for their political survival and unable or unwilling to play a global role. While the BRICS and other emerging markets have not been shy to exercise their capacity to stymie global solutions, they have not yet been prepared to play a constructive leadership role. The crisis of global leadership is in no small part associated with a dangerous period of handover. With the traditional G7 powers (typically labelled as the 'West' to the chagrin of Japan) no longer able, for financial and political reasons, to exercise leadership, and the BRICS (sometimes conflated to the 'East' or 'Asia' to the chagrin of African and Latin American countries) not yet willing or able to do so, we are drifting into a stalled period of handover in global power. That this hiatus in global power is occurring precisely at a time when issues are bubbling up that need urgent attention is a source of grave concern.

Kishore Mahbubani has written extensively about the re-emergence of Asia in global governance and the failure of the current leadership. As he has evocatively noted:

> the world has changed structurally, yet our systems for managing global affairs have not adapted. In the past, when the billions of citizens of planet earth lived in separated countries, it was like having an ocean of separate boats. Hence, the postwar order created rules to ensure that the boats did not collide; it created rules for cooperation. Up until now, this arrangement has worked well. World War III did not follow World Wars I and II. But today the world's seven billion citizens no longer live in separate boats. They live in more than 190 cabins on the same boat. Each cabin has a government to manage its affairs. And the boat as a whole moves along without a captain or a crew. The world is adrift.[132]

What is to be Done?

We have identified a range of approaches to reforming the international governance system. All of these are responses to a perceived failure identified in the earlier chapters in terms of the inability of the current system to provide: first, effectiveness in dealing with emerging global challenges and risks; second, accountability of decision-makers and legitimacy of decisions; and third, compatibility with existing institutions and values, especially with the sovereignty of nation states.

The idea that the world may be governed by international agreement was championed by the British philosopher Jeremy Bentham about two centuries ago.[133] It gradually gained traction and, following the brutal expression of nationalism after the First World War, was reflected institutionally in the creation of the League of Nations, with US President Woodrow Wilson and others enthusiastically promoting cooperation as a means of ensuring the world had experienced 'the war to end all wars'.

All international agreements require that signatories give up some sovereignty in exchange for the shared benefits of agreements. Mark Mazower, a professor of history at Columbia University, has highlighted the extent to which the European Union represents the most ambitious realization of this idea. In his view the challenges now facing the European Union raise the 'spectre of an ungovernable world' and the resurgence of sovereignty.[134]

While I am not as pessimistic as Mazower, the succession of failures of global governance to resolve critical global challenges means that a growing succession of cities—Doha, Brussels, and Rio—are now associated with stymied reforms rather than historic agreements.

Transgovernmental Networks

The potential role of transgovernmental networks as a means of increasing effectiveness and accountability in global governance has been advocated by Slaughter and others.[135] Since these networks are small and the members (generally) hold direct executive power, they should be able to act on major problems in a timely and effective fashion. Networks do not produce binding decisions and involve no delegation of power—they allow policy to be coordinated across many actors, for the benefit of all. Legitimacy and accountability are therefore derived through domestic democratic institutions, and sovereignty is not threatened.

The challenge is to ensure that they are not toothless. They are a means of establishing 'norms' of conduct that constrain the actions of states and, through the exercise of 'soft' power, could encourage compliance. Networks also offer a flexible structure that can easily adapt to new challenges. Multisectoral networks can be understood as an attempt to realize the power of connecting like-minded individuals and groupings, rather than simply nation states. They are designed to complement rather than replace existing institutions, and should offer some degree of flexibility, effectiveness, and legitimacy.

Any additional gains are the result of increased coordination. Most strategies for dealing with emerging challenges require cooperation between the private, public, and civil-society sectors. Broad consultation should therefore foster efficiency.

'Global issue networks' are a specific type of multisectoral network proposed by Rischard.[136] He argues for the creation of one network per 'global challenge', with each network developing from a small base of like-minded experts to include a wider community of stakeholders and then the capacity to monitor and evaluate. This is anticipated to create reputational incentives to improve performance. By increasing the availability of information, the implementation phase should also produce electoral incentives for states to improve performance.

This approach does not produce binding commitments, and therefore does not limit state sovereignty. According to its proponents, the open structure of global issue networks and the wide consultation process should ensure legitimacy. Effectiveness depends on the extent to which league tables and other devices to generate peer pressure produce incentives for individual states to cooperate.

Civil Society

Scholte and others have argued that increased consultation with civil-society groups could ameliorate the problems of legitimacy, accountability, and effectiveness identified above.[137] Civil-society groups can act as public educators, and can be used to gauge the political viability of particular proposals. They are uniquely placed to monitor compliance with official resolutions, and they can potentially improve accountability. A framework could be devised to ensure that civil-society groups are transparent. Provided that consultation involves representatives of all the important stakeholders and is conducted on a fair basis, the outcomes may be perceived as more legitimate. Since consultation does not involve the creation of binding commitments, this approach is seen as being compatible with national sovereignty.

Civil-society groups are powerful in many of the more democratic societies, but in the Middle East, China, and much of Africa their potential to work independently and provide a powerful source of pressure and accountability for government is limited.

Working with civil society can prove to be a boon for global campaigns and support the achievement of many of the challenges discussed in this book. However, the term covers the full range of organizations, including some, such as those mobilizing against climate change, whose global networks seek to undermine and limit global governance.

Cosmopolitan Multilateralism

While the above approaches are specifically designed to limit intrusions on state sovereignty, cosmopolitan multilateralism argues specifically for increased executive powers of multilateral institutions. This approach is justified as being the only way to ensure that global challenges are effectively dealt with and that decisions are legitimate.

Held is among those who argue that the approaches outlined above are, at most, short-term solutions.[138] Horizontal network structures will aid coordination, but will be unable to deal with problems that involve significant conflicts of interest. Unless more formal institutional structures are put in place, networks will be dominated by powerful governments and large corporations. They will therefore fail to be effective or legitimate.

The advocates of cosmopolitan multilateralism do not support the creation of a world government. Instead, they place great weight on the principle of equivalence. All individuals who are significantly affected by the presence or absence of a global public good should have the right to representation in decisions affecting its provision. Decisions should be made in the smallest possible units that include all the relevant interests. Each individual would therefore be a member of several overlapping democratic communities. Each multilateral institution would be charged with determining policy with regard to goods that affect all of and only their constituents. When significant conflicts take place, referendums determine policy. This limited extension of executive power ensures that sovereignty is maintained where possible, but that legitimacy and effectiveness take precedence when necessary.

Do We Need New Global Institutions?[139]

The crisis in global financial markets, rising concerns regarding climate change, and a range of successive global challenges, have each provoked proposals for better global institutions. How should we assess these ideas? This book has shown that faced with new threats emerging from climate change, security crises, threats of global terrorism and cybercrime, pandemics, increased migration, and financial crises, global governance is crucial. The stakes for getting it right have never been so high.

The omens are not good. If past decades provide a guide, new problems will be thrown at old institutions, created for other purposes. The UN, IMF, World Bank, and others are overloaded and cannot deliver on their mushrooming mandates. The G7—a small, informal directorate for managing the global economy that emerged in the 1970s—covers all of these issues, but its membership was a powerhouse thirty years ago and is now out of date, with the G20 exercising far more legitimacy. These and other inter-government networks, such as the G24 or G77 groups of developing countries, have neither the authority, nor the capacity, nor the legitimacy, to deliver on the enormous expectations placed on them.

Global action is important. I have shown that globalization, population and economic growth, and technological progress create growing interdependence, complexity, and fragility. But some core principles are required to guide as to when, where, and how global action is required. My Oxford colleague Ngaire Woods and I have devised the following.

First, not all issues require global collective action. A principle of subsidiarity must apply, as many are resolvable at the national, regional, or bilateral level, or by non-government actors such as the private sector or civil organizations. Those advocating a greater role for civil society or professional networks are right, up to a point. Global management must be considered only where public action pursued by governments in cooperation with one another is necessary to address the problem. More stringently, a failure on the part of governments to act collectively in a timely way would have to have dramatic and irreversible consequences.

Climate change is an obvious example where, even assuming rapid global action, the IPPC projects a temperature rise of 2 to 3 per cent, which would be catastrophic to many millions of people.[140] Global collective action is required to protect the common good. That said, as long as overall national targets are met, the principle of subsidiarity means that nation states and even communities should be able to determine how global rules are adapted to local priorities.

Second, a principle of selective inclusion is required. Key actors must be engaged and these must include not only countries with the most power to effect solutions, but also countries most affected by the problem.

Not all actors need to be involved in every global negotiation, but those that are most significant must be. In the case of climate change, this means it is essential that the twenty countries accounting for over 80 per cent of the emissions are included. Equally, however, countries most affected (such as Bangladesh, in the case of climate change) need to be included in the planning and shaping of global action. Only this will ensure a definition of the problem and design of actions that will be effective and legitimate. Top-down decision making, as reflected in IMF conditionality, the invasion of Iraq, or hand-outs by donors, is not sustainable. It also means that some existing institutions fail this test: crucial actors such as China are not members of what is now the G8 (changing from the G7 in 1997 when Russia was added), the International Energy Agency, or the International Organization for Migration, and as long as such countries are absent these institutions cannot resolve the global questions they face.

Third, a principle of variable geometry must be applied. The process of global management must be an efficient one. Nostalgia for efficiency already hangs heavily over the G8. Eight leaders sitting around a lunch table is manageable, 192 members of the UN is not. The process of global management needs to accommodate the minimum number of countries required at each stage of managing a problem. In negotiations on climate change, Tuvalu and the Alliance of Small Island States need not be represented in discussions over how emissions should be reduced, but their input is crucial to discussions on what actions are necessary to deal with irreversible changes. Effective global management will require variable geometry, or different countries engaging on different issues, and at different stages of global action.

Fourth, global management requires legitimacy. This is regularly voiced but seldom defined. Put simply, the rules of engagement in global action have to be understandable and acceptable by most countries. The test of the most basic form of legitimacy is a simple one: does a government that finds itself disadvantaged by the application of a rule, nevertheless continue to accept the rules as a whole? Presented with a 'red card', will they obey the rules or continue to participate regardless, and what authority can be exercised to force them to follow the rules of the game?

Finally, for global action to be effective there must be some degree of enforceability at the global level. Governments must do what they promise. This is not easy in a world with no single power centre. Inter-governmental reviews and pressure among governments is one route towards enforcement. Equally vital are wider public pressures which emerge when inactions or failure are brought to light by the media, by the campaigning of NGOs, or by other public institutions. This requires widespread information about what governments agree among themselves and about their compliance with the rules. The enforceability of global action therefore requires a high degree of transparency.

These five principles suggest a clear route through the crowded terrain of global governance. The world's top policy makers should confine global management to those actions that can meet the basic standards of necessity, legitimacy, and enforceability. Global action is necessary in key areas. But beware of calls for actions that fail to meet these principles—the likelihood is that leaders are simply passing along problems, not solving them collectively.

The importance of limiting global governance to those areas which absolutely require it is highlighted by Dani Rodrik. He argues for the need for nations to determine their own future free from the shackles of global institutions. He concludes that we require only a 'thin layer of simple, transparent, and commonsense traffic rules' to regulate globalization.[141] While sharing many of Rodrik's concerns regarding the dominance of existing global institutions, particularly over developing countries, the examples presented in this book point to the need for greater global governance of the new challenges, not less. As I have highlighted, the problem is that existing institutions have failed to evolve. Not surprisingly, they suffer from major failures of effectiveness and legitimacy in coping with 21st-century challenges.

We do not need a greater number of global institutions. We need radical reform of those that exist, including their streamlining. This may well involve the closure of some and the redefinition and transformation of others. Mark Malloch-Brown, the former Deputy-Secretary General of the UN, in his illuminating account of his experience, has written that a revolution is already under way in global governance and can be seen in a 'new set of commitments among people, states, and international institutions'.[142] This is an optimistic interpretation of the current morass which bedevils global problem-solving. Rather than the 'unfinished global revolution' that he identifies, I see a growing frustration among citizens with the slow progress and erosion of legitimacy and effectiveness of global governance which has gone hand-in-hand with the retreat of many national governments from global commitments.

Although they do not, in my view, amount to evidence of a revolution, Malloch-Brown is right to highlight the significance of shared global commitments such as the Millennium Development Goals or the business Global Compact as a major step forward in global governance. These agreements reflect new approaches to the global challenge of poverty which have served to enhance the effectiveness of existing institutions and engage civil society and business in new ways.

Hale and Held catalogue the failure of global institutions to address key challenges and highlight the role of transnational networks in filling the vacuum in critical areas.[143] Global networks of government officials and other committed individuals and organizations may contribute in important ways, such as in the setting and policing of regulatory standards. However, as shown in Chapter 3, they are not a panacea and have not proved effective at substituting for global agreements. Recent experience of the systemic failures of professional bodies to enforce standards in the media, in accounting, and in banking points to the need for a deep reflection on the regulatory and surveillance role of professional networks. Corporate social responsibility and business codes should be applauded and strengthened, but are not in themselves a substitute for national and global governance which carries the force of law and regulation.

The answer does not necessarily lie in more regulation, but rather in ensuring that regulators focus on the most critical challenges that are of systemic importance. This is likely to imply radical reform of the mandates, capacities, and enforcement capabilities of regulators in order that they take on national and international responsibilities which ensure the coordination of a number of systemically significant dimensions of globalization.

Regulation implies an agreed set of rules and procedures for governing conduct which, if necessary, has the force of law. The strengthening and global coordination of such rules would go a long way to managing the challenges outlined in this book.

In the End

Global politics is gridlocked. There can be no doubt that the system needs radical reform. The establishment of a shared system of rules to promote inclusive and sustainable globalization is urgently needed. The question is whether this will be in time to proactively address systemic global crises, or whether reform must emerge from the ashes of a devastating crisis, as has been the historical norm. I have argued that the financial crisis is only the first of what will be an increasingly severe set of destabilizing shocks in the 21st century. New institutions will emerge out of these crises, just as the key elements of our current institutional structure—including the UN and the Bretton Woods institutions—rose phoenix-like from the Second World War. The urgency of global governance lies in the hope that the collective management of our global commons can prevent human tragedy and suffering on a scale that may well exceed the loss of human life associated with the First and Second World Wars, Spanish influenza, and the Great Depression which scarred the last century.

When faced by the prospect of falling over an abyss, politicians do make brave decisions. The financial crisis in the European Union has demonstrated the extent to which tough and at times even politically suicidal decisions have been taken by politicians in Greece and Spain in order to escape the crisis confronting their societies. The question is whether this can be achieved in a proactive manner at the global level. Can we overcome the governance deficit before we suffer a succession of crises that would not only reverse the extraordinary achievements of recent decades, but potentially have even more devastating consequences than the disasters that beset humanity in the past century?

I am an optimist. I believe in the creative power of humanity. Physical and virtual connectivity has led to the most rapid economic and social progress humanity has ever known. It provides unprecedented opportunity to collaborate and innovate. From the crumbling of ideological and economic walls could come a century which, for the first time, is characterized by a world free of poverty and disease, resting on a shared commitment to manage our global commons. Increasing numbers of people also know it could be the most destructive century ever, where we manage to destroy not only the progress of recent centuries, but also the environment that underpins life on our planet.

This book has not aimed to provide a comprehensive compendium of global governance questions and the known responses. Rather, it has sought to stimulate thinking and through illustrative examples to suggest ways in which the global governance challenges of the 21st century are new and how we need to adapt to them. My hope is that it will encourage readers to engage in questions of global governance and, through so doing, to contribute to new solutions to this, our most urgent and complex challenge.

NOTES

Chapter 1

1 See BBC (2012).
2 For a discussion of this see Goldin and Vogel (2010).
3 Lucas (2003).
4 Securities Industry and Financial Markets Association (SIFMA) (2012).
5 World Bank (2012), GDP per capita growth.
6 See Goldin and Reinert (2012), pp. 80–112.
7 Centers for Disease Control and Prevention (2009).
8 *Washington Post* (2009).
9 World Health Organization (2009a).
10 World Health Organization (2009b).
11 World Health Organization (2009c).
12 World Health Organization (2010) and <http://www.news-medical.net/news/20120628> (last accessed 28 June 2012).
13 Johnson and Mueller (2002), pp. 105–15.
14 See Price-Smith (2009).
15 See Price-Smith (2009).
16 World Economic Forum (2011).
17 Centre For Aviation (CAPA) (2011).
18 World Health Organization (2011).
19 Barnett and Whiteside (2002), p. 4.
20 World Health Organization and UNAIDS (2011).
21 United Nations (2004).
22 Davis (2006).
23 Davis (2007).
24 See Goldin et al. (2011).
25 Estimate by author based on analysis in Goldin et al. (2011).

26 For sources and a full discussion of these issues see Goldin et al. (2011).

27 Goldin et al. (2011), p. 182.

28 Ratha (2007).

29 Anderegg et al. (2010).

30 Government Office for Science (2011).

31 IPCC (2007), pp. 173–210.

32 See ICE-SAR (2012).

33 See *CRIEnglish* (2010).

Chapter 2

34 United Nations (2011).

35 Suggested in Stern (2007).

36 *Economist* (2012).

37 See, for example, Levine (2010), pp. 196–213; and Rajan (2010).

38 Global Commission on International Migration (2005).

39 See *Guardian* (2008); and *Hindustan Times* (2011).

40 Goldin et al. (2011), p. 282.

41 Goldin et al. (2011), p. 218.

42 See, for instance, Hellwig (2009).

43 United Nations (2011).

44 Stern (2007).

45 See United Nations Security Council Resolutions (2009).

46 United Nations (2012).

47 IMF (2012).

48 This point has been made in a personal communication to the author by a Governor of the IMF.

49 *Trading Economics* (2012).

50 *Guardian* (2009).

51 PBL Netherlands Environmental Assessment Agency (2011).

52 *Time* (2007).

53 Koenig-Archibugi and Zürn (2006), p. 16.

54 Katzenstein (2005).

55 Goff (2008), pp. 213–30.

56 Thakur and Langenhove (2008), p. 25.

57 Personal communication to author from a participant at the 2012 G20 Heads of State meeting.

58 Bhagwati (1999).

59 Mansfield and Milner (2005).

60 See European Commission (2011).

Chapter 3

61 Kell (2012).

62 Buchanan and Keohane (2006).

63 *Huffington Post* (2012).

64 Goldin (2012).

65 Lamy (2012).

66 Bourguignon, Stern, and Stiglitz (2012).

67 Lamy (2012).

68 Berlin (1958). In 'Two Concepts of Liberty' he distinguishes between 'freedom to' versus 'freedom from', seen as individual liberty; he was not commenting on questions of state sovereignty.

69 Keohane and Nye (1998); and Nye (1990).

70 Slaughter (2005). See p. 12 for example.

71 Slaughter (2005), p. 12.

72 Slaughter (2005), p. 2.

73 *Time* (2003).

74 See Barrett (2007); and World Health Organization (1982).

75 Holbrooke and Garrett (2008).

76 Holbrooke and Garrett (2008).

77 Holbrooke and Garrett (2008).

78 Garrett (2009a).

79 Garrett (2009b). Interview with James Traub at the Council on Foreign Relations.

80 This recurring list is Slaughter's (2005).

81 Keohane and Nye (1998).

82 Slaughter (2005).

83 *Telegraph* (2011a).

84 See Goldin and Reinert (2012) for a discussion of this issue.

85 Publish What You Pay (2012). 'If companies disclose what they pay, and governments disclose their receipts of such revenues, then members of

civil society in resource-rich countries will be able to compare the two and thus hold their governments accountable for the management of this valuable source of income.'

Chapter 4

86 *Telegraph* (2011b).
87 *Wall Street Journal* (2012); and *Forbes* (2012).
88 BBC (2011a).
89 Department of Energy and Climate Change (2012).
90 See Crafts (1999).
91 This project of the Oxford Martin School Programme on Computational Cosmology has taken off to include millions of volunteers on a wide range of crowd-sourced projects.
92 Netcraft (2011).
93 Dawson (2009).
94 Zittrain (2008).
95 Anderson (2010).
96 *OhmyNews* (2004).
97 Sifry (2011).
98 *BBC* (2008a).
99 *BBC*(2008b).
100 Dervis (2012).
101 *Social Capital Blog* (2012).
102 *BBC* (2011c).
103 DeLong-Bas (2011).
104 *New York Times* (2011).
105 Google Crisis Response (2012).
106 Soros (2008).
107 *RFI English* (2011).
108 *Daily Mail* (2011).
109 *Guardian* (2011f).
110 Financial Tracking Service (2010).
111 *Guardian* (2011a); Wikipedia (2011).
112 One Campaign (2011).
113 Shirky (2003).
114 *Reuters* (2010).

115 Ribeiro (2011).

116 Wikipedia (2012).

117 *New York Times* (2012).

118 *Guardian* (2011b); and (2011d).

119 *BBC* (2011b).

120 *Guardian* (2011c); and (2011e).

121 ICE-SAR (2012).

122 See ATL (2004).

123 Council on Foreign Relations (2006).

124 Geopolity (2011).

125 OECD: Somer and Brown (2011).

126 *BBC* (2005).

127 The *Nation* (2009).

Chapter 5

128 Barrett (2007).

129 Osborne (2011).

130 See Goldin and Reinert (2012).

131 Lamy (2012).

132 Mahbubani (2011) in *The New York Times*.

133 This paragraph draws on Mazower (2012).

134 Mazower (2012).

135 Slaughter (2005).

136 Rischard (2002).

137 Scholte (2004).

138 Held (2005), pp. 10–27.

139 This section draws heavily on a joint OpEd, 'Do We Need New Global Institutions? Five Guiding Principles', I drafted in collaboration with Ngaire Woods, to whom I am most grateful both in terms of her contribution and for helping to clarify my thinking on these points.

140 IPCC (2007).

141 Rodrik (2011), p. 280.

142 Malloch-Brown (2011), p. 241.

143 Hale and Held (2012).

BIBLIOGRAPHY

Anderegg, W. R. L., Prall, J. W., Harold, J. and Schneider, S. H. 2010. 'Expert Credibility in Climate Change'. *Proceedings of the National Academy of Sciences*. Published ahead of print 21 June 2010. <http://www.pnas.org/content/early/2010/06/04/1003187107.full.pdf+html> (last accessed 5 April 2012).

Anderson, C. 2010. 'How Web Video Powers Global Innovation'. *TED*. September. <http://www.ted.com/talks/chris_anderson_how_web_video_powers_global_innovation.html> (last accessed 19 April 2012).

ATL. 2004. 'Company Primer on Preparedness and Response Planning for Terrorist and Bioterrorist Attacks'. *Business Executives for National Security*. <http://www.scribd.com/doc/57116207/ATLWhitePaper-022004> (last accessed 20 April 2012).

Barrett, S. 2007. *Why Cooperate? The Incentive to Supply Global Public Goods*. Oxford: Oxford University Press.

Barnett, T. and Whiteside, A. 2002. *AIDS in the Twenty-first Century: Disease and Globalization*. Basingstoke: Palgrave Macmillan.

Biermann, F. and Gupta, A. 2011. 'Accountability and Legitimacy in Earth System Governance: A Research Framework'. *Ecological Economics*, 70(11), pp. 1856–64.

BBC. 2005. 'Cruise Lines Turn to Sonic Weapon'. 8 November 2005, <http://news.bbc.co.uk/1/hi/world/africa/4418748.stm> (last accessed 20 April 2012).

BBC. 2008a. 'Oil Contract Scandal Shakes Peru'. 7 October 2008, <http://news.bbc.co.uk/1/hi/world/americas/7656500.stm> (last accessed 5 April 2012).

BBC. 2008b. 'Oil Row Brings Down Peru Cabinet'. 10 October 2008, <http://news.bbc.co.uk/1/hi/world/americas/7664803.stm> (last accessed 5 April 2012).

BBC. 2011a. 'Teenager Arrested on Suspicion of Hacking'. 21 June 2011, <http://www.bbc.co.uk/news/technology-13859868> (last accessed 5 April 2012).

BBC. 2011b. 'England Riots: Twitter and Facebook Users Plan Clean-up'. 9 August 2011, <http://www.bbc.co.uk/news/uk-england-london-14456857> (last accessed 5 April 2012).

BBC. 2011c. 'Tunisia Unveils Bouazizi Cart Statue in Sidi Bouzid'. 17 December 2011, <http://www.bbc.co.uk/news/world-africa-16230773> (last accessed 5 April 2012).

BBC. 2012. 'World Leaders: Nuclear Terrorism a "Grave Threat"'. 27 March 2012, <http://www.bbc.co.uk/news/world-asia-17520156> (last accessed 5 April 2012).

Berlin, I. 1958. 'Two Concepts of Liberty' in Isaiah Berlin. 1969. *Four Essays on Liberty*. Oxford: Oxford University Press.

Bhagwati, J. 1999. 'Regionalism and Multilateralism: An Overview', in J. Bhagwati, P. Krishna, and A. Panagariya, (eds.), *Trading Blocs: Alternative Approaches to Analyzing Preferential Trade Agreements*. Massachusetts: MIT Press, pp. 3–32.

Bhagwati, J. 2008. *Termites in the Trading System: How Preferential Agreements Undermine Free Trade*. Oxford: Oxford University Press.

Bloomberg Business Week. 2012. 'Jamie Dimon's Risky Business'. 14 June 2012, <http://www.businessweek.com/articles/2012-06-14/jamie-dimons-risky-business> (last accessed 15 June 2012).

Bourguignon, F., Stern, N., and Stiglitz, J. 2012. 'End the Monopoly: Let's make it a Real World Bank at Last'. *Financial Times*. 18 March 2012.

Buchanan, A. and Keohane, R. 2006. *The Legitimacy of Global Governance Institutions*. Princeton: Princeton University Press.

Centre For Aviation (CAPA). 2011. 'World Airport Rankings 2010: Big Changes to Global Top 30. Beijing Up to #2, Heathrow Falls to #4'. 16 March 2011, <http://www.centreforaviation.com/analysis/world-airport-rankings-2010-big-changes-to-global-top-30-beijing-up-to-2-heathrow-falls-to-4-47882> (last accessed 17 April 2012).

Centers for Disease Control and Prevention. 2009. 'Morbidity and Mortality Weekly Report. Outbreak of Swine-origin Influenza A (H1N1) Virus Infection—Mexico, March-April 2009'. <http://www.cdc.gov/mmwr/preview/mmwrhtml/mm58d0430a2.htm> (last accessed 16 April 2012).

Council on Foreign Relations. 2006. 'Sarin'. <http://www.cfr.org/weapons-of-terrorism/sarin/p9553> (last accessed 10 September 2012).

Crafts, N. 1999. 'Economic Growth in the Twentieth Century'. *Oxford Review of Economic Policy*, 15(4), pp. 18–34.

CRIEnglish. 2010. 'Chinese Team Offers Aid in Haiti'. 15 January 2010, <http://english.cri.cn/6909/2010/01/15/45s542729.htm> (last accessed 5 April 2012).

Daily Mail. 2011. 'Société Générale'. 9 August 2011, <http://www.dailymail.co.uk/money/markets/article-2024243/Soci-t-G-n-rale.html> (last accessed 5 April 2012).

Davis, J. 2007. 'Hackers Take Down the Most Wired Country in Europe'. *Wired Magazine*, 15(09), <http://www.wired.com/politics/security/magazine/15-09/ff_estonia> (last accessed 5 April 2012).

Davis, M. 2006. *Planet of Slums*. London: Verso.

Dawson, C. 2009. 'Ubuntu a Minor Player? Not Outside the States'. *ZDNet*. 17 June 2009, <http://www.zdnet.com/blog/education/ubuntu-a-minor-player-not-outside-the-states/2709> (last accessed 16 April 2012).

DeLong-Bas, N. 2011. 'The New Social Media and the Arab Spring'. *Oxford Islamic Studies Online*, <http://www.oxfordislamicstudies.com/Public/ed_advisors.html#akhavi> (last accessed 5 April 2012).

Department of Energy and Climate Change. 2012. 'Carbon Offsetting'. <http://www.decc.gov.uk/en/content/cms/emissions/co2_offsetting/co2_offsetting.aspx> (last accessed 5 April 2012).

Dervis, K., 2012. 'The Economic Imperatives of the Arab Spring'. *Project Syndicate*. 12 January 2012.

Economist. 2012. 'Mathematics and Epidemiology: Neighbourly Advice'. 23 January 2012, <http://www.economist.com/blogs/babbage/2012/01/mathematics-and-epidemiology?fsrc=scn/tw/te/bl/neighbourlyadvice> (last accessed 5 April 2012).

European Commission. 2011. 'The Common Agricultural Policy Explained'. *European Commission Directorate-General for Agriculture and Rural Development*. Available at <http://ec.europa.eu/agriculture/publi/capexplained/cap_en.pdf> (last accessed 20 March 2012).

Financial Times. 2012. 'Decline of Global Institutions Means We Best Embrace Regionalism'. 27 January 2012.

Financial Tracking Service. 2010. 'Haiti Funding Received'. <http://fts. unocha.org/reports/daily/ocha_Rreportf_A893_asof___1209101534 .pdf> (last accessed 10 September 2012).

Forbes. 2012. 'JP Morgan's London Whale Losses Could Hit £9 Billion'. 28 June 2012, <www.forbes.com/sites/steveschaefer/2012/06/28> (last accessed 29 June 2012).

Garrett, L. 1995. *The Coming Plague: Newly Emerging Diseases in a World out of Balance.* London: Penguin.

Garrett, L. 2009a. 'The Path of a Pandemic'. *Newsweek.* 1 May 2009.

Garrett, L. 2009b. 'The Global Response to the Swine Influenza'. Interview with James Traub, *Council on Foreign Relations.* 8 May 2009. New York. Transcript available at <http://www.cfr.org/health-and-disease/global-response-swine-influenza/p19399> (last accessed 19 April 2012).

Geopolity. 2011. 'The Economics of Piracy: Pirate Ransoms and Livelihoods off the Coast of Somalia'. May 2011, <http://www.geopolicity. com/upload/content/pub_1305229189_regular.pdf> (last accessed 5 April 2012).

Global Commission on International Migration. 2005. 'Migration in an Interconnected World: New Directions for Action. Report of the Global Commission on International Migration'. Available at <http:// www.gcim.org> (last accessed 5 April 2012).

Goff, P. 2008. 'Making Cultural Policy in a Globalising World' in A. Cooper, C. Hughes, and P. De Lombaerde (eds.), *Regionalisation and Global Governance: The Taming of Globalisation?* London: Routledge, pp. 213–30.

Goldin, I. 2012. 'The World Bank is Flirting with Irrelevance'. *Financial Times.* 5 March 2012.

Goldin, I., Cameron, G., and Balarajan, M. 2011. *Exceptional People: How Migration Shaped Our World and Will Define Our Future.* Princeton, NJ: Princeton University Press.

Goldin, I. and Reinert, K. 2012. *Globalization for Development: Meeting New Challenges.* Oxford: Oxford University Press.

Goldin, I. and Vogel, T. 2010. 'Global Governance and Systemic Risk in the 21st Century: Lessons from the Financial Crisis'. *Global Policy,* 1 (1), pp. 4–15.

Google Crisis Response. 2012. See <http://www.google.org/crisisresponse/ index.html> (last accessed 20 April 2012).

Government Office for Science. 2011. 'Foresight: Migration and Global Environmental Change: Future Challenges and Opportunities. Final Project Report'. London.

Guardian. 2008. 'Paradise Almost Lost: Maldives Seek to Buy a New Homeland'. 10 November 2008.

Guardian. 2009. 'Why We Need a World Environment Organisation'. 28 October 2009.

Guardian. 2011a. 'Japan Crisis: Should NGOs Launch Emergency Appeals?'. 17 March 2011.

Guardian. 2011b. 'London Riots: How BlackBerry Messenger Played a Key Role'. 8 August 2011.

Guardian. 2011c. 'London Riots: Police to Track Rioters Who Used Black-Berrys'. 9 August 2011.

Guardian. 2011d. 'Rights Groups Uneasy Over Cameron's Riot Crack-down'. 13 August 2011.

Guardian. 2011e. 'Facebook Riot Calls Earn Men Four-year Jail Terms Amid Sentencing Outcry'. 16 August 2011.

Guardian. 2011f. 'Google Plus Forces Us to Discuss Identity'. 30 August 2011.

Hale, T. and Held, D. 2012. 'Gridlock and Innovation in Global Governance: The Partial Transnational Solution'. *Global Policy* 3(2), pp. 169–81.

Held, D. 2005. 'Principles of the Cosmopolitan Order' in G. Brock and H. Brighouse (eds.), *The Political Philosophy of Cosmopolitanism*. Cambridge: Cambridge University Press, pp. 10–27.

Held, D. and Koenig-Archibugi, M. (eds.) 2005. *Global Governance and Public Accountability*. Oxford: Blackwell.

Hellwig, M. 2009. 'Systemic Risk in the Financial Sector: An Analysis of the Subprime Mortgage Financial Crisis'. *De Economist* 157(2), pp. 129–207.

Hindustan Times. 2011. 'Sinking Maldives Would Like to Buy Land in India'. 13 September 2011.

Holbrooke, R. and Garrett, L. 2008. '"Sovereignty" That Risks Global Health'. *Washington Post*, 10 August 2008.

Huffington Post. 2012. 'Flu Pandemic, Climate Pattern May Be Linked'. 17 January 2012.

Hurrell, A. 2007. *On Global Order: Power, Values, and the Constitution of International Society*. Oxford: Oxford University Press.

ICE-SAR. 2012. *The Icelandic Association for Search and Rescue.* Available at <http://www.icesar.com/> (last accessed 19 April 2012).

IMF. 2012. 'IMF Executive Directors and Voting Power'. <http://www.imf.org/external/np/sec/memdir/eds.aspx> (last accessed 5 April 2012).

IPCC. 2007. 'Freshwater Resources and their Management. Climate Change 2007: Impacts, Adaptation and Vulnerability. Contribution of Working Group II to the Fourth Assessment Report of the Intergovernmental Panel on Climate Change'. Cambridge: Cambridge University Press, pp. 173–210.

Johnson, N. P. and Mueller, J. 2002. 'Updating the Accounts: Global Mortality of the 1918–1920 "Spanish" Influenza Pandemic'. *Bulletin of the History of Medicine,* 76(1), pp. 105–15.

Katzenstein, P. J. 2005. *A World of Regions: Asia and Europe in the American Imperium.* Ithaca, NY: Cornell University Press.

Kell, G. 2012. 'Time to Bring Corporate Sustainability to Scale'. *International Institute for Sustainable Development,* 20 March 2012. Available at <http://www.unglobalcompact.org/docs/news_events/in_the_media/IISD_20.3.12.pdf> (last accessed 19 April 2012).

Keohane, R. and Nye, J. 1998. 'Power and Interdependence in the Information Age'. *Foreign Affairs,* 77(5), pp. 81–94.

Koenig-Archibugi, M. and Zürn, M. 2006. *New Modes of Governance in the Global System: Exploring Publicness, Delegation and Inclusiveness.* Basingstoke: Palgrave Macmillan.

Lamy, P. 2012. 'Global Governance Local Governments', Distinguished Public Lecture, 8 March 2012. Oxford: Oxford Martin School.

Lan, T. and Nagorski A. 2010. *Global Cyber Deterrence: Views from China, the U.S., Russia, India, and Norway.* New York: EastWest Institute.

Levine, R. 2010. 'An Autopsy of the US Financial System: Accident, Suicide or Negligent Homicide'. *Journal of Financial Economic Policy,* 2(3), pp. 196–213.

Lucas, R. 2003. *Macroeconomic Priorities.* Department of Economics, University of Chicago. Available at <http://oldweb.econ.tu.ac.th/archan/chaiyuth/New%20growth%20theory%20Review%20in%20Thai/macro%20perspectives_lucas.pdf>.

Mahbubani, K. 2011. 'A Rudderless World'. *New York Times,* 18 August 2011, <http://www.nytimes.com/2011/08/19/opinion/19iht-edmahbubani19.html> (last accessed 10 September 2012).

Malloch-Brown, M. 2011. *The Unfinished Global Revolution*. London: Penguin.

Mansfield, E. and Milner, H. 2005. 'The New Wave of Regionalism', in P. Diehl (ed.), *The Politics of Global Governance: International Organizations in an Interdependent World*. Boulder, Co: Lynne Rienner, pp. 330–73.

Mazower, M. 2012. 'Europe Raises the Spectre of an Ungovernable World'. *Financial Times*. 25 May 2012.

Medical News. 2012. 'Swine-flu Deaths Far Greater than Reported'. 28 June 2012, <www.news-medical.net/news/20120628> (last accessed 29 June 2012).

Nation. 2009 'The Cost of Doing Business on the Open Sea'. 22 April 2009, <http://www.thenation.com/article/cost-doing-business-open-sea> (last accessed 5 April 2012).

Netcraft. 2011. 'May 2011 Web Server Survey'. Available at <http://news.netcraft.com/archives/2011/05/02/may-2011-web-server-survey.html> (last accessed 5 April 2012).

New York Times. 2010. 'Digital Help for Haiti'. 27 January 2010.

New York Times. 2012. 'After an Online Firestorm, Congress Shelves Antipiracy Bills'. 20 January 2012.

Nye, J. 1990. 'Soft Power'. *Foreign Policy*, 80, pp. 153–71.

OhmyNews. 2004. 'A Marriage of Democracy and Technology'. 15 December 2005. Available at <http://english.ohmynews.com/articleview/article_view.asp?no=201599&rel_no=1> (last accessed 14 April 2012).

One Campaign. 2011. 'Key Findings from the DATA Report 2011'. 13 May 2011, <http://one.org/data/blog-en/2011/05/key-findings-from-the-data-report-2011/> (last accessed 5 April 2012).

Osborne, G. 2011. 'Together We Will Ride Out the Storm'. *Conservative Party Conference*. 3 October 2011. Full speech available at <http://www.conservatives.com/News/Speeches/2011/10/Osborne_together_we_will_ride_out_the_storm.aspx> (last accessed 23 April 2012).

PBL Netherlands Environmental Assessment Agency. 2011. *Climate Change Dossier*. Available at <http://www.pbl.nl/en/dossiers/climatechange/faqs#vraag8> (last accessed 19 April 2012).

Price-Smith, A. 2009. *Contagion and Chaos: Disease, Ecology, and National Security in the Era of Globalization*. Cambridge, MA: MIT Press.

Publish What You Pay. 2012. See <http://www.publishwhatyoupay.org/about/faqs> (last accessed 19 April 2012).

Rajan, R. 2005. 'Has Financial Development Made the World Riskier?'. *Proceedings, Federal Reserve Bank of Kansas City,* August 2005, pp. 313–69.

Rajan, R. 2010. *Fault Lines: How Hidden Fractures Still Threaten the World Economy.* Princeton, NJ: Princeton University Press.

Ratha, D. 2007. 'Leveraging Remittances for Development'. *Migration Policy Institute Policy Brief,* June 2007. Washington, DC: Migration Policy Institute.

Reuters. 2010. 'Analysis: WikiLeaks Battle: A New Amateur Face of Cyber War?'.9 December 2010.<http://www.reuters.com/article/2010/12/09/us-wikileaks-cyberwarfare-amateur-idUSTRE6B81K520101209> (last accessed 20 April 2012).

RFI English. 2011. 'European Markets Recover, UK Paper Apologises for Société Générale Rumours'. 11 August 2011. Available at <http://www.english.rfi.fr/asia-pacific/20110811-european-markets-recover-uk-paper-apologises-societe-generale-rumours> (last accessed 19 April 2012).

Ribeiro, J. 2011. 'Anonymous Claims Hack of Texas Police Website. *PC World.* 2 September 2011, <http://www.pcworld.com/businesscenter/article/239407/anonymous_claims_hack_of_texas_police_website.html< (last accessed 20 April 2012).

Rischard, J. F. 2002. *High Noon: 20 Global Problems, 20 Years to Solve Them.* New York: Basic Books.

Rodrik, D. 2011. *The Globalization Paradox: Why Global Markets, States and Democracy Can't Coexist.* Oxford: Oxford University Press.

Scholte, J.A. 2004. *Democratizing the Global Economy: The Role of Civil Society.* Coventry: CSGR.

Securities Industry and Financial Markets Association (SIFMA) (2012). 'Global CDO Issuance and Outstanding (xls)—quarterly data from 2000 to Q1 2012 (issuance), 1990—Q1 2012 (outstanding)'. 12 April 2012, <http://www.sifma.org/uploadedFiles/Research/Statistics/StatisticsFiles/SF-Global-CDO-SIFMA.xls> (last accessed 16 April 2012).

Shirky, C. 2003. 'A Group Is Its Own Worst Enemy'. Available at <http://shirky.com/writings/group_enemy.html> (last accessed 20 April 2012).

Sifry, M. 2011. *WikiLeaks and the Age of Transparency.* New Haven: Yale University Press.

Slaughter, A. 2005. *A New World Order.* Princeton, NJ: Princeton University Press.

Social Capital Blog. 2012. 'Twitter, Facebook and You Tube's role in the Arab Spring'. Updated 3 February 2012, <http://socialcapital.wordpress.com/2011/01/26/twitter-facebook-and-youtubes-role-in-tunisia-uprising/> (last accessed 5 April 2012).

Somer, P. and Brown, I. 2011. 'Reducing Systemic Cybersecurity Risk'. *OECD Project. Future Global Shocks*. 14 January 2011, <http://www.oecd.org/dataoecd/57/44/46889922.pdf> (last accessed 5 April 2012).

Soros, G. 2008. *The New Paradigm for Financial Markets*. New York: Public Affairs Press.

Stern, N. 2007. 'The Stern Review: The Economics of Climate Change'. *Cabinet Office—HM Treasury*. January 2007.

Telegraph. 2011a. 'Sony Says 25m More Users Hit in Second Cyber Attack'. 3 May 2011.

Telegraph. 2011b. 'City Rogue Trader Kweku Adoboli Arrested over $2bn UBS Loss'. 15 September 2011.

Time. 2003. 'Doing Battle with the Bug'. 7 April 2003.

Time. 2007. 'Indonesia's Bird Flu Showdown'. 10 May 2007.

Thakur, R. and Langenhove, L. V. 2008, 'Enhancing Global Governance through Regional Integration' in A. Cooper, C. Hughes, and P. De Lombaerde (eds.), *Regionalisation and Global Governance: The Taming of Globalisation?* London: Routledge, pp. 17–43.

Trading Economics. 2012. 'United States Unemployment Rate'. Available at <http://www.tradingeconomics.com/united-states/unemployment-rate> (last accessed 5 April 2012).

United Nations. 2004. 'World Population to 2300. Department of Economic and Social Affairs Population Division'. New York. Available at <http://www.un.org/esa/population/publications/longrange2/WorldPop2300final.pdf> (last accessed 17 April 2012).

United Nations. 2011. 'Millennium Development Goals Indicators'. Available at <http://mdgs.un.org/unsd/mdg/SeriesDetail.aspx?srid=749&crid=> (last accessed 19 April 2012).

United Nations. 2012. 'Member States. Growth in United Nations Membership, 1945–Present'. Available at <http://www.un.org/en/members/growth.shtml> (last accessed 5 April 2012).

United Nations Security Council Resolutions. 2009. Available at <http://www.un.org/documents/scres.htm> (last accessed 19 April 2012).

Wall Street Journal. 2012. 'J.P. Morgan Knew of Risks'. 12 June 2012, <http://online.wsj.com/article/SB10001424052702303768104577460792166155830.html> (last accessed 12 June 2012).

Washington Post. 2009. 'New Strain of Swine Flu Investigated: Two Children in San Diego Area Had No Contact With Pigs'. 22 April 2009, <http://www.washingtonpost.com/wp-dyn/content/article/2009/04/21/AR2009042103694.html> (last accessed 16 April 2012).

Wikipedia. 2011. 'Humanitarian Response to the 2011 Tōhoku Earthquake and Tsunami'. Available at <http://en.wikipedia.org/wiki/Humanitarian_response_to_the_2011_T%C5%8Dhoku_earthquake_and_tsunami> (last accessed 5 April 2012).

Wikipedia. 2012. 'English Wikipedia Anti-SOPA Blackout'. Available at <http://wikimediafoundation.org/wiki/English_Wikipedia_anti-SOPA_blackout> (last accessed 5 April 2012).

World Bank. 2012. 'GDP Per Capita Growth (Annual %)'. Available at <http://data.worldbank.org/indicator/NY.GDP.PCAP.KD.ZG/countries/1W?display=graph> (last accessed 5 April 2012).

World Economic Forum. Blanke, J. and Chiesa, T. (eds.) 2011. *The Travel & Tourism Competitiveness Report 2011: Beyond the Downturn.* Geneva, Switzerland.

World Health Organization. 1982. 'Archives of the Smallpox Eradication Programme, a Guide and Inventory'. Vol. 2. Geneva.

World Health Organization. 2009a. 'Swine Influenza—Update 4'. *Global Alert and Response (GAR).* 28 April 2009, <http://www.who.int/csr/don/2009_04_28/en/index.html> (last accessed 16 April 2012).

World Health Organization. 2009b. 'Influenza A(H1N1)—Update 44'. *Global Alert and Response (GAR).* 5 June 2009, <http://www.who.int/csr/don/2009_04_28/en/index.html> (last accessed 16 April 2012).

World Health Organization. 2009c. 'Pandemic (H1N1) 2009—Update 67'. *Global Alert and Response (GAR).* 20 September 2009, <http://www.who.int/csr/don/2009_04_28/en/index.html> (last accessed 16 April 2012).

World Health Organization. 2010. 'Pandemic (H1N1) 2009—Update 100'. *Global Alert and Response (GAR).* 14 May 2010, <http://www.who.int/csr/don/2009_04_28/en/index.html> (last accessed 16 April 2012).

World Health Organization. 2011. 'HIV/AIDS Data and Statistics'. Available at <http://www.who.int/hiv/data/en/> (last accessed 11 June 2012).

World Health Organization and UNAIDS. 2011. 'Global Summary of the AIDS Epidemic 2010'. Available at <http://www.who.int/hiv/data/2011_epi_core_en.png> (last accessed 11 June 2012).

Woods, N. 2006. *The Globalizers: The IMF, the World Bank, and their Borrowers*. Ithaca, NY: Cornell University Press.

Zittrain, J. 2008. *The Future of the Internet—And How to Stop It*. New Haven: Yale University Press.

INDEX